MW01699674

Estate Planning Handbook

Third Edition

William P.G. Allen
B.A., LL.M.

John P. Allen
B.A., B.Sc., LL.B.

CARSWELL
Thomson Professional Publishing

The paper used in this publication meets the minimum requirements of American National Standard for Information Sciences — Permanence of Paper for Printed Library Materials, ANSI Z39.48-1984.

Canadian Cataloguing in Publication Data

Allen, William P.G.
Estate planning handbook

3rd ed.
Includes index.
ISBN 0-459-26020-0

1. Inheritance and succession — Canada — Handbooks, manuals, etc.
2. Estate planning — Canada — Handbooks, manuals, etc. I. Allen, John Pearson, 1961- II. Title.

KE806.A764 1999 346.7105'2 C99-931406-8
KF750.A76 1999

CARSWELL
Thomson Professional Publishing

One Corporate Plaza, 2075 Kennedy Road, Scarborough, Ontario M1T 3V4
Customer Care:
Toronto and International 1-416-609-3800
Elsewhere in Canada/U.S. 1-800-387-5164
Fax 1-800-298-5094

To Doris and Meredyth.

Preface

Fourteen years have gone by since the first edition of this handbook was published, eight years since the second edition.

Much has happened since the first edition, such as legislation regarding family law; substitute decision making, trustee investing, taxation. Computers have changed the way documents are prepared, stored, and transmitted.

Family structure has changed. People now define, and redefine, their families. Remarriages, common-law relationships, single parents, children born outside marriage, personal animosities – all of these, and more, mean that each person, when defining persons in a class or group who are to benefit from a testamentary or inter-vivos trust, pays less regard to "legitimate" blood relationships. People redefine their "families" as their relationships change.

Economic classes are changing. The distinction between "haves" and "have-nots" continues. The distinction between the self-employed and those who work for organizations is growing sharper; different estate planning considerations are beginning to apply to each.

Much has not changed - the person, and not assets, at the centre of estate planning; the need for clear thinking and writing, the need to ease the transfer of assets and their management from one person and generation to another.

Our thanks to our families for their patience while we prepared this edition; and our special thanks to Sheila Crummey, and to Tom Allen, lecturer in law, Durham University, England, one of the authors of the second edition, for his corrections and suggestions.

June, 1999 William Allen and John Pearson Allen

Contents

Introduction

This 3rd edition, like the earlier handbooks, gathers together some important elements of estate planning, as a quick and, we hope, easy guide.

We have divided this book into parts:

- In Part I, we describe the usual tools of estate planning: the trust, the powers of attorney for property and for personal care, the Will, the contract, the corporation, life insurance.
- In Part II, we discuss some planning considerations: the administration of an estate, family law considerations, incapacity, taxes.
- In Part III, we discuss some common planning situations: the young family, the second marriage, the family business.
- In Part IV, we discuss plain language, and include some precedents, with comments in them on how to use them.

The precedents are "building blocks" – plain language suggestions for particular situations. Too often, it seems, long precedents are imported, the document expands, and the reader is distracted and confused. There is a principle of physics that a gas fills the available space. Today, documents are longer, more technical, as if compelled to fill the capacity of our word-processors.

"I just want a simple Will. I just have the house and the pension. Everything is to go to my wife, and if she dies, the kids. What's so complicated about that? Why is your draft Will so long? Why do you have all this extra stuff in there?"

Develop an outline - perhaps in order from general to specific, or in chronological order, or from significant to trivial assets. Complete the plan before starting the draft. You'll receive better instructions, and your time will be appreciated. Focus on the important, gather your thoughts, develop a theme, and unfold it with your reader in mind. A good legal document is about the people involved, and answers the who? what? when? where? and why? questions.

Focus on the important - The Why?

Why is the document being prepared? What are your client's objectives? Ask open-ended questions so your client tells you what's important. Later, you can focus on specifics, and ask about contingencies.

Gather your thoughts

Who?

Who is your reader? Obviously in a Will, the testator has to understand what he or she is signing, but what about the executor and the beneficiaries? Is the document too technical? Will it help the survivors to deal with the situation and finances, or will it only confuse and contribute to a loss of control?

Who are the parties and beneficiaries? For example, in a Will, does the testator want to include her adopted children? Her grandchildren born now or also those born later? In a shareholders' agreement, is there a significant creditor who should also be a party?

What?

What is to happen? For example, are the trustees to divide assets equally among the beneficiaries, or should they give more to the one who needs more? Should they invest only in safe investments, or should they accept risks to gain more in the long run?

What is to happen to the house? To the cottage? To the family business?

When?

When do the obligations of the document begin? For example, when is the trust fund to be divided among the children? When the oldest is age 25 or when the youngest is age 21?

Where?

Where does the document apply? What about property in Florida? the children in Vancouver? and what about the original marriage contract made in Quebec?

Part I
Tools

1

The Trust

TRUST DEFINED

A trust is where one person holds legal title to property for the use of another.

A "trust" is not a separate entity like a corporation, but the *relationship* between the holder of the property, the "trustee", and the person for whom the property is being held, the "beneficiary". Assets are transferred to a trustee, not to a trust.

Yet the trust is more than the relationship. Beneficial rights attach to the property, imposing the trust on any subsequent legal owner with notice of the trust. So if the trustee dies, or if legal ownership to property is transferred or lost, the beneficiary retains the beneficial interest in the property even though the relationship with the original trustee is altered or extinguished.

USING A TRUST

Trusts are created either by a person's intention, or imposed by a statute or court. A "testamentary" trust is an intentional trust created by Will; an "inter-vivos" trust is an intentional trust created during a person's lifetime.

Intentional trusts are used in two situations: Firstly, where the person who is to receive the property is not suited to full ownership, temporarily or permanently (perhaps because of age, illness, financial inexperience, or potential exposure to creditors). Secondly, to give to one person (or a group of people) the use of the property (physical use, or the income) for a time, and then to give the property to another (or a group of people) later.

Having accepted the appointment, the trustee must follow the terms of the trust and cannot be released until either the beneficiary or court approves.

FORMING THE TRUST

The contributor of property to an intentional trust is the "testator" in the case of a testamentary trust, and the "settlor" in the case of an inter-vivos trust.

An inter-vivos trust is settled either by declaration or by transfer.

If the trust is settled by declaration, the settlor continues to own the property and declares that its use is for another. No particular form is necessary, and no document need be witnessed or under seal.

If the trust is settled by a transfer of property to another as trustee, then the transfer itself must be valid and complete, with the trustee ending up with the property. For example, if the trust is created by Will, the formalities of a valid Will must be satisfied. If the trust is created by an inter-vivos gift, the formalities of a valid gift must be satisfied, and if the trust is created by contract, the formalities of a valid contract must be satisfied.

The Three Certainties of a Trust

Courts speak of the "three certainties" of a trust: certainties of intention, subject matter, and object(s).

Certainty of Intention

The settlor must intend to impose trust obligations on the person receiving the property. Difficulties arise when the settlor uses words suggesting only an intention to guide, such as "I wish" or "I desire". It is best to state clearly when no binding obligation is intended. For example, if the settlor gives money to a school to buy a set of ency-clopaedias, the following is clear:

> "I suggest that the school use the funds to buy a set of encyclopaedias for the students; however, this is just a recommendation and it is not intended to bind the school."

The Trust Property (Certainty of Subject Matter)

The assets of the trust must be identified, or there must be a method of identifying them.

For example, "set aside sufficient money to maintain John Smith at his current standard of living for ten years" is a valid trust, provided that John Smith's current standard of living can be determined.

The Beneficiaries (Certainty of Objects)

A settlor can create a trust to benefit persons, or to benefit purposes.

In a trust for persons, the beneficiaries must be identified, or identifiable, with certainty. Obviously, the trust is certain if the beneficiaries are named.

What if the beneficiaries are described as a class of persons, such as "my family", "my friends", or "my grandchildren who are married when I die"? In all cases, the trustee must be able to determine whether any particular person is a member of the class. In some cases, the trustee must also be able to determine who *all* the members of the class are. It depends on whether the trust is discretionary or non-discretionary.

In a *discretionary* trust, the trustee need not know who all the members of the class are before distributing, provided a reasonable number are known. For example, "give $1,000 to those of my friends who you, my trustee, decide need winter clothes." Because the trustee need not give winter clothes to all of the settlor's needy friends, she can start giving $1,000 to those friends who presently need winter clothes, without knowing all the friends.

In a *non-discretionary* trust, the second test is required - the trustee must be able to determine all the members of the class. For example, "give an equal share of the fund to my friends who survive me." In this case, unless the trustee can determine who all of the deceased's surviving friends are, the trustee won't know what an equal amount is.

Trusts for Purposes

Traditionally, only persons could be beneficiaries of a trust, because only a person can appear in court in an action against the trustee. Abstract purposes, such as "use $1,000 to improve the quality of air" are not enforceable trusts, since "air" could never sue the trustee. Examples of failed purpose trusts include: trusts for research into the production of a new alphabet, for the training of journalists and the improvement of newspapers, and for the erection of a suitable memorial to a deceased relative.

However, trusts for recognized public charities are exempt from the rule because the Public Trustee, on behalf of the public, has standing to enforce charitable purposes.

What if the settlor wishes to benefit a non-charitable purpose? An avoidance of the rule is to give to members of an association committed to a purpose, rather than giving to the abstract purpose itself. For example:

> "Give $10,000 to the Pickering hockey association; I ask that the fund be used to improve minor hockey".

This is a valid gift because the beneficiaries are the members of the association and the request that the funds be used for hockey skills is only a request.

DRAFTING THE TRUST

Like any legal document, consider the who? what? when? where? and why? questions.

Why the Trust?

Why is the trust being prepared? What is its purpose? Is it to shield the young, elderly, or incapable, from the management of property? Is it to retain value until the children are older? Will it hold special assets, such as a business or cottage? Is it for a tax purpose, such as an estate freeze?

Draft the trust, and consider its language and technicalities, with its purpose and reader in mind.

What is the Trust Property?

What is the trust property? Does it match the purpose of the trust? Will it be difficult or time-consuming to administer?

What kind of investments are suitable? An investment might produce a generous income, but no capital gain; or a generous capital gain, but no income. Unless the document states otherwise, the *Trustee Act* lists appropriate investments. They tend to be conservative, well-secured investments - mostly bonds and preferred shares of public companies.

Who are the Beneficiaries?

Who are the beneficiaries? Should the choice of beneficiaries be postponed? If postponed, describe the "class" or group from which they will be chosen and indicate how those choices should be made.

Power to Appoint Beneficiaries

The settlor can retain or give someone else (including the trustee), the power to appoint who is to receive trust property. Giving the power of appointment to someone other than the trustee may be useful. For example, the settlor may wish to provide for her grandchildren, and give her child the power to determine how much each grandchild should receive and when, without having her child act as trustee or manage or control the property.

(When drafting powers of appointment, keep in mind the *Family Law Act* (Ontario) and the *Income Tax Act* . The value of property subject to a power that the donee can exercise in favour of the donee is included in the donee's net family property. And, if the settlor reserves a power to appoint - whether to appoint to the settlor or to someone else - the income and capital gains of the fund may be attributed back to the settlor.)

When Does the Class of Beneficiaries Close?

When does the class gift "close", i.e. when are the members of the class to be determined? For example, in a bequest "to A for life, then equally to my grandchildren", which grandchildren share the gift - those who survive the testator, or those who survive A? What about grandchildren who survive the testator, but die before A - do their descendants share in the gift?

Problems are avoided by clear wording. Instead of "to A for life, then equally to my grandchildren", consider the following:

"To A for life, then equally among my grandchildren who survive A"

- The class of grandchildren closes when A dies. All grandchildren who survive A will share.

"To A for life, then equally to my grandchildren, and their descendants by representation, who survive A"

- The class of grandchildren and their descendants closes when A dies. All grandchildren who survive A will share; the descendants who survive A of a grandchild who dies before A will share in the portion of their deceased parent.

Who are the Trustee(s)?

Match the trustee(s) with the purpose, property and beneficiaries of the trust. Should a trustee have a financial background, or be familiar with business or tax issues? Should a trustee be the manager of the family business? Should a trustee be from the family?

The settlor can be the trustee, or one of a group of trustees.

The settlor can retain the power to terminate a trustee, to appoint a replacement trustee, to appoint more trustees, or one, both, or all of these. Or, the settlor can give these powers to someone else.

How will Decisions be Made?

Trustees must act unanimously, unless the document says otherwise. Some trusts allow a majority of trustees to make decisions. If a settlor wants to avoid the rule of unanimity but maintain a veto over the trust, she could appoint herself as trustee and say that only a majority that includes herself may make decisions.

All the trustees are responsible for everything that is done, unless the trust says otherwise. If the trustees allow one of their number to manage and control the fund, they are still all responsible. They cannot be passive, unless the trust says otherwise.

Trustees cannot delegate their responsibilities, though they should seek advice from experts (they may be under a duty to do so) or hire others to carry out administrative duties.

How is the Property to be Shared?

How is the property to be shared among current beneficiaries, and among succeeding classes of beneficiaries? A trustee must not favour one beneficiary over another, except as the trust document allows. Where there are succeeding income and capital interests, the trustee must produce a reasonable income without exposing the capital to undue risk.

Should the document describe the sharing, or should the trustee have discretion? Should the trustee have the power to encroach on the capital for the income beneficiary? (In spousal trusts, where the spouse has the income for life and the children, perhaps by a prior marriage, are entitled to the capital when the spouse dies, guidance on exercising discretions might prevent the trustee from becoming involved in a family dispute.)

When will the Trust End?

When will the trust end? When will the property be distributed to the beneficiaries?

A trustee, or someone else (including the settlor), can be given the power to decide when to distribute. For example:

> "The balance of the fund shall be paid to my nephew John when he reaches 35, or at such earlier date as his mother shall appoint". (The full clause would contain a gift over because of the rule in *Saunders v. Vautier* noted below; also the trust should deal with the income up to the final distribution. If necessary, special conditions could be put on the exercise of the power.)

When must the Trust End?

Premature Termination of the Trust - Saunders v. Vautier

In Ontario, if all the beneficiaries of a trust are ascertained, and if none are under a legal disability (including minority), they can have the trust wound up and the trust property distributed to them as they see fit, because they together "own" the entire right of enjoyment in the trust property. This is known as the rule in *Saunders v. Vautier* (1841), 4 Beav. 115; 41 E.R. 482. The beneficiaries can invoke the rule without the approval of the court or of the trustees, even if it is contrary to the apparent intention of the settlor.

A common problem is when a trust fund is left for a minor child and the document says that the capital is not to be paid to the child until an age over maturity, for example, at 25. Unless the testator includes a condition to the child receiving the capital at 25, the child will be entitled to claim the capital at 18. In this case, the settlor can include a gift over to another person or persons if the beneficiary dies before reaching 25. For example, instead of saying "to A when he reaches 25", say "to A when he reaches 25, but if he does not reach 25 then to B".

Rule Against Perpetuities

There is a rule against the indefinite postponement of vesting, to prevent testators from controlling assets too long - it favours the living as against the dead.

An interest must vest within 21 years after the death of someone who is alive when the interest is created and whose life describes the time for the vesting. An interest is vested if the person to receive it is ascertained, or known, and the person need only wait to receive it. If the person dies in the meantime, their estate will receive the property.

> "To X when she reaches 21"
> X's interest is vested; she receives possession at 21. (If X dies before 21, X's estate receives the property).

> "To X for life, then to Y"
> X's life interest is vested; Y's interest is also vested; she receives possession when X dies. (If Y dies before X, then Y's estate receives on X's death).

An interest is contingent if the person receives the property only if something happens (the "condition precedent"). If the event does not happen, the person and their estate do not receive the property.

> "To X if she survives me"
> X may or may not outlive the testator, meantime, while the testator lives, her interest is contingent. (If X dies before the testator, then X's estate does not inherit).

> "To X for life, then to Y if Y survives X"
> Y may or may not outlive X. While X lives, Y's interest is contingent. (If Y dies before X, then Y's estate does not inherit. X's life interest is vested.)

"To X for life, then to my children who survive X"
A child may or may not survive X. Each child's interest is contingent on surviving X.

Later vesting: An interest may not be vested when the trust was created, but become vested later when an earlier person dies:

"To X if she survives me. To Y for life if Y survives X, then to Z"
(X's interest is contingent on surviving the settlor. Y's interest is contingent on surviving X. If, during the trust, Y takes the property, then Z's interest *becomes* vested.)

In some cases, it is clear that the interest vests within the perpetuity period and the interest is valid. In other cases, it is clear that the interest can only vest outside the perpetuity period and the interest is invalid. Under the Ontario *Perpetuities Act,* if the timing of vesting is uncertain, the interest is presumed valid until events establish the contrary - the "wait and see" principle. In a class gift, if the members' interests may vest beyond the perpetuity period, then "wait and see"; if it is later found that some potential beneficiaries prevent others from vesting within the period, the non-vesting beneficiaries are excluded.

The Income - The Accumulations Act

The indefinite accumulation of income in a trust is considered to be against the public interest. Income accumulation exists if a trustee is directed or permitted to retain income without distributing it. The *Accumulations Act* allows income to be accumulated for one, and only one, of the following periods (the settlor may choose which one of these periods will apply to the trust):

1. the life of the grantor of the property;
2. 21 years from making an inter-vivos disposition;
3. the duration of the minority or respective minorities of any person or persons living or conceived but not born at the date of making an inter-vivos disposition.;
4. 21 years from the death of grantor, settlor, or testator;
5. the duration of the minority of a person living or unborn at the death of grantor, settlor, or testator;
6. the duration of the minority of a person who would have been entitled to the income, but for his minority.

If a direction or power to accumulate contravenes the Act, the income which would have accumulated after the chosen period goes to the persons who would have been entitled had it been paid out.

One way of avoiding the rule is by directing the trustees to pay out the income if and when required to do so by the Act. For example, in a testamentary trust that pays 25% of the annual income to a child, the following would avoid the accumulation rules:

> "Pay 25% of the annual income to my child, and add the balance to capital. However, if this fund is still continuing twenty-one years after I die and if required by the law of accumulations to do so, starting twenty-one years after I die and after my child reaches majority, pay all the annual income of the fund to my child."

2

The Continuing Power of Attorney for Property

A "power of attorney for property" is where one person is authorized to deal with the property of another. The attorney (who need not be a lawyer) is the "agent" and the owner of the property is the "principal".

The "power" is only a discretion; the attorney need not exercise it - however, once exercised, the attorney becomes a "fiduciary". The attorney does not hold legal ownership and is not liable for the contracts or debts incurred. The attorney is merely a conduit between principal and third party, contracting "for", "per", or "on behalf of" the principal.[1]

The attorney can be given the power to manage property ("administrative powers") or the power to choose who is to receive the property on a distribution ("distributive powers"). The power may be limited to specific purposes (signing an agreement to sell a property, selling a security), or it may be a general power (to do anything that the principal can do). Normally, the power does not authorize the attorney to make gifts on the principal's behalf.

A single power may appoint more than one attorney - jointly, severally, or both. A substitute attorney can be named. More than one power can be outstanding. (Some stationer's forms include a paragraph revoking all previous powers of attorney - this should be deleted if several powers are intended.)

---

1 This is unlike a trust. The trustee *must* follow the terms of the trust. The trustee holds the legal or "title interest" of the property for the beneficiary; contracts directly with third parties and is personally liable on those contracts (the trustee can recover from the trust property, but the third party is not concerned with this).

CONTINUING POWER OF ATTORNEY

Normally, the power of attorney ends on the incapacity of either the principal or attorney, on the theory that it is an ongoing authorization, and once either is dead, bankrupt, or mentally incompetent, the authorization ends. (This is unlike a trust, in which the settlor transfers property to the trustee - if the settlor dies or becomes incapable, the trustee continues to hold the property for the beneficiary and follow the terms of the trust.)

However, the Ontario *Substitute Decisions Act* recognizes the "continuing power of attorney". This is a power which continues after the incapacity of the principal. It can authorize the attorney to do anything in respect of the property that the principal could do, except make a Will or replace the principal in some fiduciary capacity. To grant the continuing power of attorney, the principal must:

1. know what kind of property he or she has and its approximate value;
2. be aware of obligations owed to his or her dependants;
3. know that the attorney will be able to do anything in respect of property that the principal could do if capable, except make a Will, subject to the conditions and restrictions set out in the power of attorney;
4. know that the attorney must account for his or her dealings with the property;
5. know that he or she may, if capable, revoke the continuing power of attorney;
6. appreciate that unless the attorney manages the property prudently its value may decline; and
7. appreciate the possibility that the attorney could misuse the authority given to him or her.

Two witnesses are required. They cannot be: (1) the attorney or the attorney's spouse or partner; (2) the principal's spouse or partner; (3) a child of the principal or a person whom the principal has demonstrated a settled intention to treat as his or her child; (4) a witness whose property is under guardianship or who has a guardian of the person; or (5) a witness who is less than eighteen years old.

The continuing power of attorney may take effect when signed, on a specified date, or when a contingency occurs. If the contingency is the incapacity of the principal, and if the document does not provide a method for determining the principal's incapacity, then the power takes effect when:

1. the attorney is notified by a provincially designated assessor that the assessor has found the principal incapable of managing property; or
2. the attorney is notified that a certificate of incapacity has been issued under the *Mental Health Act*.

The continuing power of attorney ends when:

1. The principal dies;
2. The attorney dies, becomes incapable of managing property or resigns, unless there is another attorney authorized to act or there is a substitution created by the power of attorney;
3. The court appoints a guardian of the property of the principal - see Chapter 10 on "Incapacity";
4. The principal executes a new continuing power of attorney for property (unless there are to be multiple powers of attorney); or
5. The power of attorney is revoked - a revocation must be in writing and must be executed in the same way as a continuing power of attorney for property. Many powers of attorney include a clause revoking earlier powers.

How does an Attorney under a Continuing Power Resign?

The attorney can resign, but if he or she has taken any action under the power of attorney, the resignation does not take effect until a copy of the resignation is delivered to the principal, to any other attorneys named in the power of attorney, and to the person named as a substitute for the attorney who is resigning.

When the attorney is resigning, if he or she believes that the principal is incapable, and there is no substitute attorney, the attorney must also deliver the resignation to the principal's spouse (or partner), and to the relatives known to the attorney who live in Ontario. The resigning attorney also notifies persons with whom the attorney is dealing on the principal's behalf.

Duties of the Attorney under a Continuing Power (Agent)

- Act in the principal's best interests;
- Manage the property consistent with decisions concerning the person's personal care;
- Consult with the principal, and with those who take care of the person, and with the person's family and friends;
- Use what there is, first, for the person's support and care; then if assets are available, for the dependants; then for other obligations;
- If there is something left over, the attorney can make gifts or loans to relatives, and gifts to charity based on her previous practice. Gifts to charity cannot be more than 20% of income unless the power says otherwise;
- Obtain a copy of the person's Will and information about their assets and liabilities. If, in the Will, there is a bequest of a particular asset, do not dispose the asset unless necessary; if so, the person who was to receive it is to have an equivalent value from the estate;
- Keep accounts;
- Keep copies of the continuing power of attorney and of any related court orders; and
- Keep matters confidential.

ACCOUNTS

The attorney must keep accounts and provide an accounting when asked to do so. The regulations require the attorney to keep:

1. a list of all the incapable person's assets as of the date of the first transaction, including real property, money, securities, investments, motor vehicles and other personal property;
2. an ongoing list of assets acquired and disposed of on behalf of the incapable person, including the date of and reason for the acquisition or disposition and from or to whom the asset is acquired or disposed;
3. an ongoing list of all money received on behalf of the incapable person, including the amount, date, from whom it was received, the reason for the payment and the particulars of the account into which it was deposited;

4. an ongoing list of all money paid out on behalf of the incapable person, including the amount, date, purpose of the payment and to whom it was paid;
5. an ongoing list of all investments made on behalf of the incapable person, including the amount, date, interest rate and type of investment purchased or redeemed;
6. a list of all the incapable person's liabilities as of the date of the first transaction by the attorney or guardian on the incapable person's behalf;
7. an ongoing list of liabilities incurred and discharged on behalf of the incapable person, including the date, nature of and reason for the liability being incurred or discharged;
8. an ongoing list of all compensation taken by the attorney or guardian, if any, including the amount, date and method of calculation;
9. a list of the assets, and value of each, used to calculate the attorney's or guardian's care and management fee, if any.

How Much will the Attorney under a Continuing Power be Paid?

The power of attorney can state how much the attorney will be paid. If it doesn't, and if the attorney wants payment, the fees will be prescribed by regulation. At present, the fees are 2 ½ per cent on capital and income receipts; 2 ½ per cent on capital and income disbursements; and two-fifths of 1 per cent on the annual average value of the assets as a care and management fee.

What Happens if There is No Continuing Power of Attorney?

See Chapter 10 on "Incapacity".

3

The Power of Attorney for Personal Care

A "power of attorney for personal care" is where one person is authorized to make personal care decisions for another when the other becomes incapable. Personal care decisions include medical treatment decisions (therapeutic, preventive, palliative, diagnostic and other health-related treatment); decisions about whether to move to a nursing home or care facility; decisions about nutrition and hygiene; decisions about safety; decisions about clothing and recreation; and decisions about social services provided to the person.

No personal care decision can be made for adults (even if the decision-maker is appointed under a power of attorney for care) unless they are incapable of making the decision for themselves. (This is different than a power of attorney for property, which can take effect while the grantor is still capable.) Someone is incapable of making personal care decisions if:

1. For medical treatment decisions, the person is "not able to understand the information that is relevant to making a decision about the treatment, admission or personal assistance service, as the case may be, and is not able to appreciate the reasonably foreseeable consequences of a decision or lack of decision."
2. For all other decisions, where there are reasonable grounds to believe that the grantor is incapable of making the decision. In addition, a power of attorney can require an independent assessment of capacity before the attorney can make decisions.

Many people want restrictions in their power of attorney regarding "heroic efforts" to prolong life - the "living will". However, even if the health practitioner receives a copy of the patient's wishes and is aware of their general attitude to treatment, an informed consent to the specific treatment is still required (from the person or their substitute decision maker), unless it is an emergency. If it is an emergency, then the last known wishes of the patient are followed, but the treatment may be continued only until a consent can be obtained. Therefore, rather than rely on living wills which, in a sense, can become stale, treatment choices should be discussed in advance with those will make the personal care decisions on their behalf - i.e. the attorney, family and physician.

DUTIES OF THE ATTORNEY

Attorneys must explain their powers and duties to the incapable persons, and must follow the incapable person's wishes; if the wishes have not or cannot be expressed, then according to their best interests - these include the values and beliefs that the person would act on if capable, and that are known to the attorney.[1]

The attorney must choose the least restrictive and intrusive course of action that is available and is appropriate.

The attorney shall, as far as possible, foster the person's independence, and shall encourage the person to participate, to the best of his or her abilities, in the decisions made. The attorney should also foster regular personal contact between the person and their supportive family members and friends.

RECORDS OF DECISIONS

The attorney shall keep the following records:

1. a list of all decisions regarding health care, safety and shelter made on behalf of the incapable person, including the nature of each decision, the reason for it and the date;
2. a copy of medical reports or other documents, if any, relating to each decision;

---

1 Prior to the March 1996 amendments to the *Substitute Decisions Act*, the personal care attorney had to explain the necessity for the personal decision; if the person objected, the power had to be "validated". This required an application to the Public Guardian and Trustee, an assessment by two assessors confirming the incapacity, and a government appointed advocate giving "rights advice" to the person and then confirming that the person does not object to the validation.

3. the names of any persons consulted, including the incapable person, in respect of each decision and the date;
4. a description of the incapable person's wishes, if any, relevant to each decision, that he or she expressed when capable and the manner in which they were expressed;
5. a description of the incapable person's current wishes, if ascertainable and if they are relevant to the decision;
6. for each decision taken, the attorney's opinion regarding the incapable person's best interests.

WHO CAN BE APPOINTED AN ATTORNEY FOR CARE?

Anyone, except someone who is paid to provide health care or residential, social, training or support services to the person, unless he or she is their spouse, partner or relative.

CAN MORE THAN ONE ATTORNEY BE APPOINTED?

Yes, two or more attorneys for personal care can be appointed. They must act jointly, unless the power says otherwise. If one of the attorney dies, becomes incapable or resigns, unless the power says otherwise, the remaining attorney(s) can act.

WHEN DOES THE POWER OF ATTORNEY FOR CARE END?

It ends if the attorney dies or becomes incapable or resigns, unless there is another joint attorney or there is a substitute attorney. It also ends if a new power of attorney for personal care is signed, unless the new power provides that there shall be multiple powers of attorney for personal care. It also ends if the court appoints a guardian of the person (see Chapter 2).

WHAT HAPPENS IF THERE IS NO POWER OF ATTORNEY FOR CARE?

See Chapter 10 on "Incapacity".

4

The Will

A Will is a written and signed statement, made by an individual, disposing of property on death. To be valid in Ontario, it must be either a holograph Will (wholly handwritten and signed by the testator), or it must be witnessed by two persons who are neither beneficiaries under the Will nor married to beneficiaries. The Will must be signed while the testator is mentally competent and not "unduly" pressured.

DRAFTING THE WILL

Structure

Draft the Will with the executor in mind and consider the phases of the administration of an estate (see Chapter 8, "Estate Administration"). In the first phase, the executor assembles the deceased's assets, pays the debts and administration costs, and distributes what is left to the beneficiaries. The executor has a reasonable time for this (sometimes called the "executor's year").

If there are ongoing trusts to administer, then there is a second phase (which can last for many years). There may be a trust for the spouse for life, or a trust for a child until a stated age, or there may be a trust for a parent. The trustee can be the executor, or someone else.

Know Your Client

It is more than simply listing the assets and liabilities, reviewing prior Wills, and listing the family. Learn what the testator thinks of the spouse. Should conditions be imposed on the beneficiaries? It is a profound thing to contemplate one's death, and how others will survive the loss.

Know What Will Work

Know what will work legally and what will work practically. Does the plan help some at the expense of others? If the asset values shrink, will the legacies, taxes, and costs consume the residue? Does the plan divide the family?

Keep It Simple

A complicated plan is more likely to fail. The survivors need to know where they stand, and how to get the funds to continue their lives. All estates require timely attention. Good prices and opportunities can be lost if the plan is too complicated for those left to manage it.

Prepare an Outline

Prepare an outline and review it with your client before embarking on a long draft. As always, consider who? what? when? where? and why? questions.

LIST THE ASSETS AND LIABILITIES

What are the Assets?

Make a list of the assets - the house, cottage or farm, investments, pensions and savings plans, and life insurance.

Who are the beneficiaries named in life insurance policies and savings plans - the spouse or the estate? Are there personal things - jewellery, art - of special value?

Has the testator loaned money to the family? Does the testator expect to receive something when a relative dies? Does the testator have an interest in a private business?

How is Title Held?

Is the title to real estate in the testator's name, in the spouse's name, or both? Does the joint owner take the property by right of survivorship?

Even if the property is held jointly, if the contributions to the asset were unequal, the survivor may hold part of the legal interest in trust for the contributor's estate under the resulting or constructive trust doctrines (see below).

In Ontario, as between spouses, property held in their joint names is presumed to be beneficially owned jointly.

Are there Restrictions on Transferring Assets?

The right to transfer shares in a private company may be restricted by the corporation's articles, bylaws or shareholders' agreements. Partnership property could be subject to similar agreements.

Licences to use trademarks, computer software, or other property, may be personal to the testator and may be extinguished by death. Or, a consent may be needed to transfer the licence to the estate or beneficiary.

The testator may own property that has a mortgage. If so, review the mortgage to determine if the debt becomes payable as a result of the mortgagor's death.

What are the Liabilities?

Make a list of the liabilities - mortgages, bank loans, and private loans. Calculate the capital gains and other taxes that will be paid on death.

Will the Spouse Make a Claim Against the Estate?

The surviving spouse has six months to choose whether to claim his or her share of the increased net family property during the marriage, or what he or she is to receive under the Will (or if there is no Will, what is provided for by intestacy). See Chapter 9, "The Ontario Family Law Act".

Have the Dependants been Provided For?

Testators must provide adequately for the support of their dependants. A "dependant" means the spouse (including a common law spouse), child, parent, or sibling to whom the deceased was providing (or legally should have been providing) support prior to death. See Chapter 9, "The Ontario Family Law Act".

Resulting and Constructive Trusts

A resulting trust can exist when one person transfers property to (or buys property for) another person without consideration. The presumption is that the transfer was not a gift, and that the beneficial ownership remains with the transferor. (The exception, as mentioned above, is for joint property between spouses).

A constructive trust can exist if one person contributed to the value of another person's asset(s) without compensation. To remedy the unjust enrichment, the court can declare that the legal owner holds the beneficial interest in trust for the contributor.

To protect the Will against such claims, determine if anyone made a contribution to any of the testator's assets, whether in work or money, before or after the asset was acquired. If the testator does not plan to leave the asset to the potential claimant in the Will, more details are needed to determine if the asset is at risk. If so, keep the evidence for the executor.

The testator may have a claim for the property of another by a resulting or constructive trust. If so, the executor may be obliged to enforce the claim, even against the surviving spouse. Accordingly, the testator should either release the property-holder from the claim, either in the Will or separately, or provide the executor with some evidence so that the executor will have a basis from which to contest a claim.

Who will Pay the Debts?

Unless stated otherwise, the debts are paid out of the residue of the estate. Debts include income and estate taxes. However, the testator can say that a particular gift will bear the debt connected to it. For example, suppose the testator owns a property that is to go to one child (not as part of the residue) and that carries a substantial capital gains tax that will have to be paid when she dies. In the Will, the testator can charge that property with the payment of the tax.

WHO ARE THE BENEFICIARIES?

Beneficiares can be chosen outright, or trusts can be created with the power to the trustees (or to another) to later determine who shall receive from among a class.

What happens if the beneficiary dies before the testator? What if the beneficiary dies before the trust is distributed? What if the property is no longer available? Consider these, and the trust questions in Chapter 3.

What if the Spouses die in a Common Accident?

Most Wills include a "common disaster" clause, in the event both spouses die in the same accident but not at the same time (perhaps one will be on life support for a few hours or days). Otherwise, property can pass through two estates before reaching the ultimate beneficiaries.

Spousal gifts are conditional on the spouse surviving the testator by a short period, such as 30 days. This also excludes the survivorship rules under section 55 of the Ontario *Succession Law Reform Act*: where two people die at the same time, or in circumstances rendering it uncertain which of them survived the other or others, the property of each is disposed of as if he or she had survived the other, and joint tenancies held are deemed to have been tenancies in common.

Giving to a Spouse Trust

Spouse trusts are common. For example, in second marriages spouses with their own children may want the survivor to have the income from the assets of the one who dies first, and when the survivor dies, the capital is to go to their own children. Or, the person may want a trust for their spouses because the spouse may not be able to manage the assets.

Assets that should go outright to the spouse, such as the home and contents and art and personal things, should not go into a trust. Special assets, such as the home or art or the business interest, should go into special trusts dealing with those assets.

The family property elective rights of the surviving spouse may put the spouse trust at risk (see Chapter 9). Also, the survivor who is capable of managing the property and who is left a spouse trust may consider it an insult and an embarrassment. She has to ask the trustees for her entitlement. If there is a power to encroach on the capital, she has to ask the trustees for what she feels is hers without the asking. A trust for the widow may put her in the position of having to ask her children, if they are the executors, for what should be hers. Too often, widows receive what others consider she "needs". Often, a good plan will include a sizeable legacy outright to the spouse in addition to the trust. The legacy gives independence, and the trust secures the capital to the children.

Granting the Power to Later Choose Beneficiaries

The plan may give someone who is not an executor or a trustee distributive powers, such as the power to encroach on capital, or to divide income or capital among a class. Many people are willing to accept responsibility for the administration of the estate if it does not include authority to allocate benefits unevenly. Others are prepared to accept that responsibility but do not want the job of administering the estate.

Co-Ownership by Children

Children, normally, should not be expected to co-own inherited property for long. Even if they are compatible, they will have different needs and wishes. For example, a child who cannot enjoy the family cottage after the parents die, who gets no value from it, may resent the others who enjoy it every summer.

Children may resent the "favoured child" who is running the family business, who is expected to pay a portion of its value to the others, and who has discretion to manipulate cash flow. The most practical solution is to provide the child running the business a first right to purchase it, at its fair market value, with payment outright or by reduction in the child's share in the remainder of the estate (see Chapter 14, "The Family Business").

Are Adopted "Children" Included?

In Ontario, by the *Children's Law Reform Act,* a person is the child of his or her natural parents, whether born inside or outside of marriage, and a person's adoptive parents are deemed to be his or her natural parents.

Just as a child can be adopted into a family, he or she can be adopted out of a family. For example, if the testator has an unmarried or divorced son who has a child, and the child's mother has custody and marries another man, the child is still the testator's grandchild. However, if the new husband adopts the child, the child is "adopted out" of the family and is no longer the testator's grandchild.

These rules apply to the construction of a Will or other legal document, unless a contrary intention appears. So, if the testator wishes to include or exclude children, they should be specifically mentioned.

Appointing a Guardian of a Child

There are two types of guardians of the child: the guardian of the child's person and the guardian of the child's property.

Guardian of the child's person means "custody" of the child - i.e. making decisions about the child's health, education and welfare. Both parents have custody unless a court order or separation agreement says otherwise. However, where the parents live separate and apart and the child lives with one, with the implied consent or acquiescence of the other, the live-in parent has sole custody, and the other has reasonable access.

Guardian of the child's property means having charge of, and responsibility for, the care and management of the child's property until the child is age eighteen. Neither parent is the guardian of the child's property unless appointed by the court or in the Will of the previous guardian of the child's property. However, a parent with whom the child resides or who has custody of the child and who receives property for the child has the same responsibilities as a guardian.

In Ontario, the existing guardian of the person or property can, by Will, appoint the next guardian for a period of ninety days, and the person so appointed can, within the ninety days, start a new court application to continue as guardian.

It may be useful in the Will to appoint different people as the guardian of the child's person and of the child's property.

When There Isn't Enough - Abatement

When preparing the plan, be sure that there will be enough to pay the debts and taxes and the costs to administer the estate and the legacies, so there will be a remainder. If there is a shortfall, the legacies will "abate" (reduce), and the issue then becomes - who shares in the reduction? The Will can define the sharing.

When the Asset is Gone - Ademption

If the testator makes a gift of a specific asset which cannot be found after death, the gift fails, or "adeems". This applies if the asset was lost, destroyed, sold, given away, or changed into another form.

However, the rule has been modified somewhat by section 20 of the Ontario *Succession Law Reform Act*, by tracing the gift to the proceeds or security received by the testator. Also, if the asset was given away by an attorney under a continuing power of attorney, then under the *Substitute Decisions Act* the would-be beneficiary is entitled to receive from the residue of the estate the equivalent of a corresponding right in the proceeds of the disposition of the property, without interest.

If the Beneficiary Dies First - Lapse

If the Will includes a gift to someone who dies before the testator, unless a contrary intention appears in the Will, the gift fails, or "lapses".

However, section 31 of the Ontario *Succession Law Reform Act* states that, except when a contrary intention appears in the Will, a bequest to a child, grandchild, brother or sister who has predeceased the testator takes effect as if it had been made directly to the intended beneficiary's survivors.

Avoiding Partial Intestacy

Partial intestacies commonly occur in two situations:

Firstly, where a residuary beneficiary dies before the testator, and the Will does not include a gift over. Unless the anti-lapse provisions of the legislation apply, an intestacy of the residue occurs. (To avoid this, include a gift over of the residue.)

Secondly, where the distribution of capital is delayed, there is an intestacy if the Will does not say what is to be done with some or all of the income arising before the distribution. For example, in "to A when he reaches 35; before then $350 monthly to B", there is a partial intestacy of the income if it exceeds $350.

What is the "Residue"?

Use the words "remainder" and "residue" consistently in the Will. There may be several remainders, or residues, in the estate. There is the remainder of the whole estate: what is left after all the other provisions in the Will are satisfied. There is the remainder of an ongoing testamentary trust, whether the trust property consists of certain assets or of a share of the general residue. Sometimes the remainder of a particular trust is added to the general residue. Keep the distinctions clear in the Will.

Life Insurance Designations

The Ontario *Insurance Act* allows a designation by declaration in the Will. The designation takes effect as of the date of signing the Will, so a later designation, whether by Will or other document, can override the earlier designation. A designation in the Will is not necessarily invalid if the Will is invalid. If the Will is later revoked, the designation is also revoked.

The declaration should include a description of each policy, including the name of the insurer and the policy number. General declarations are not accepted by some insurance companies. A notarial copy of the Will should be sent to the insurance company before death, to confirm that the designation will be accepted.

If the testator wants the executor to use the proceeds to pay estate debts, then the estate should be designated as the beneficiary. If the insurance designation is to be made in the Will, and if the proceeds are not to pass through the estate, the designation should not be grouped with the dispositive provisions of the Will and should clearly state that it is a declaration pursuant to the *Insurance Act.*

If the testator irrevocably designates someone to receive the proceeds on death, then the proceeds are not within the control of the estate and are thus immune from the deceased's creditors. Also, the law protects the proceeds from creditors where the designation is not irrevocable, but is to a spouse, child or grandchild.

Under the Ontario *Succession Law Reform Act*, the amount payable under an insurance policy owned by the deceased is included in the value of the deceased's estate when determining the amount of support, and can be charged with the support payments.

Designations of Pensions and RRSPs

In Ontario, a plan participant can make or revoke a beneficiary designation by Will. The designation takes effect as of the date of signing the Will, so a later designation, whether by Will or other document, can override the earlier designation. A designation in the Will is not necessarily invalid if the Will is invalid. If the Will is later revoked, the designation is also revoked.

A designation in a Will is effective only if it relates expressly to a plan, either generally or specifically. Therefore, a designation in a Will does not include a plan acquired after the Will is made.

Unlike designated life insurance, no matter what the designation, the RRSP or pension forms part of the deceased's estate and is available to creditors (whether the creditors can seize the asset depends on legislation - generally, RRSPs are seizable and certain pension plans are not). In addition, under the *Succession Law Reform Act*, the amount payable under the plan is included in the value of the deceased's estate when determining the amount of support, and can be charged with the support payments.

WHO ARE THE EXECUTORS?

Consider not only the transfer of the ownership of assets, but also the transfer of management. Even in a distributable plan - where the estate goes outright to the beneficiaries after payment of the debts, difficulties or special assets may cause delay.

In the meantime, assets are managed. If there are ongoing trusts - trusts for minors or for spouses - the assets allocated to those trusts must be managed for the term of each trust. A beneficiary may need time to develop the skills to manage an asset. Or, there may be a group of beneficiaries who are to receive the asset whose management interests differ. Or, all the children may inherit a business, but only one will manage it.

Choosing the right executors and trustees is vital. Separate managers can be appointed for separate functions, to meet the needs of special assets or separate ongoing trusts for different beneficiaries. Or, the plan could require, as a pre-condition to distributing the estate, an agreement among the beneficiaries as to management.

The executors should be sensitive to the needs of the family; they should be able to do the job and to know when to get help and from whom. They should not be expected to do the clerical work; they should be permitted - indeed encouraged - to have someone else do administrative things such as keeping the accounts, doing the tax returns, and the like.

Different Executors and Trustees for Different Tasks

The plan may have different persons administer separate parts of the plan. There may be special executors for some of the assets, such as literary or artistic works, or special executors to manage and dispose of the business, or to deal with foreign assets. There may be different trustees for separate ongoing testamentary trusts. For example, the surviving parent of a deceased child may be a trustee of a grandchild's substituted share.

Separate Trusts for Special Assets

If an asset - such as the family business, the country property, the home, the art collection - needs special consideration in the plan, give it special treatment in the Will.

Some assets need special management. If the asset is to be held for a continuing purpose (such as an interest in the home for the surviving spouse, or a business to be managed for a time and then to go to one child, or a country property that will be held for the family), do not leave it in the residue of the estate. Use a special trust with special terms.

PROTECTING THE PLAN

Suspicious Circumstances, Notes

Be alert to suspicious circumstances. Is a child pressuring the parent to change the Will to favour the child at the expense of others? Is the husband pressuring the wife to do what he wants, and not what she wants? Why is the Will being changed? Is there any doubt as to the client's capacity to make or change the Will?

If there are suspicious circumstances, make notes of how they are resolved. When there is a substantial change in the client's distribution plan, know why the client wants to change, and note the reasons for the change. Note the instructions, including the assets and liabilities. If some of the assets will be difficult to administer, and if the client has suggestions, note these for the assistance of the administrator.

Keep the notes for later referral. Notes of the instructions, of the reasons for change, and of dealings with any suspicious circumstances will add to the security of the plan. Without them, if the Will or the plan is attacked after the death, the plan may fail and the lawyer could be liable for negligence.

Note who witnessed the Will and where the original is held.

Claims Against the Estate for Constructive Trusts

As noted above, to protect the Will against claims for constructive trusts, determine if anyone made a contribution to any of the testator's assets, whether in work or money, before or after the property was acquired. If the testator does not plan to leave the property to the potential claimant in the Will, more details are needed to determine if the asset is at risk. If so, keep the evidence for the executor.

REVOKING THE WILL

A Will can be revoked in writing. A later Will revokes the earlier one. It can be revoked by burning, tearing or otherwise destroying the Will. It is revoked on marriage, unless made in contemplation of marriage, or the new spouse elects to take under the Will. On divorce, any bequests or appointments to the former spouse are construed as though the former spouse predeceased the testator.

5

The Contract

A contract is a mutual exchange of promises. To be binding:

- *The parties must agree on the essential terms*: Usually, one party starts with an offer which, if accepted, becomes a contract. The offer must be intended as such - more than an invitation to consider or advertisement. The acceptance must be unconditional; a counter-offer is a rejection of the previous offer.
- *There must be an exchange of value or "consideration"*: Otherwise it is a gift, and gifts are unenforceable (except if the document is under seal.)
- *The value exchanged must be legal*: Courts do not enforce illegal acts, such as: bets, restraints of trade, or criminal promises.
- *The parties must be "legally competent"*: Minors cannot contract, except for the purchase of necessities. The mentally incapable, delirious or bankrupt cannot contract. A corporation must contract through its agents.
- *No duress or undue influence*: Actual violence or threats of violence coercing a party to enter a contract relieves the coerced party. Also, if one party is in a dominant position (such as a bank, employer, or doctor), "undue influence" may be presumed - in such cases (and especially in domestic agreements), independent legal advice should be obtained.
- *Mistakes must be innocent*: In most cases, and especially where there is no consumer protection legislation, neither party is required to disclose information to the other - "caveat emptor". So, if one side is "fooled" because of his or her failure to inquire, then the contract remains enforceable. However, where one side actively "fools" the other by distorting or suppressing material facts, then the contract can be set aside; and if the misleading was intentional, the wronged party can seek additional damages.

CONTRACTS IN ESTATE PLANNING

Contracts are often part of an estate plan.

Marriage contracts in second marriages are used to define property rights and support claims, to secure a survivor's right to occupy a home or to have specified income, and to secure capital to children if the income is to be used for the survivor.

Contracts are frequently used when planning for the succession of a family business, such as buy-sell agreements by family members. See Chapter 14, "The Family Business".

DRAFTING CONSIDERATIONS

Be wary of precedents - don't simply adopt solutions to someone else's problems.

Consider the elements of a valid agreement. In a spousal agreement with property division, is there undue duress or influence? (Each spouse should have independent legal advice, with full disclosure of all assets and liabilities.)

Do the spouses want every contingency spelled out in a marriage contract? For a second marriage with children from prior marriages, is the document really for the spouses during the marriage or to assist the surviving children on death?

Consider the variables in any contract: If the contract is based on the price of something, what happens if the price changes because of inflation, recession, or a strike? What if the law changes after the contract was signed? For example, many separation agreements required an amount of child support based on certain tax benefits. When the tax law changed by eliminating deductibility to the payor, few agreements permitted the payor to pay less child support. For each rule of law you identify, you should consider what should happen if the law changes.

Pretend you are a party hostile to the document. Try to pick it apart. Look for ambiguities to construe in your favour and identify weaknesses.

6

The Corporation

A corporation is a legal entity separate in law from its owners. The shareholders own the corporation, but not its assets and liabilities. Thus, the shareholder's liability is "limited" - should the corporation's liabilities become greater than its assets, the creditors of the corporation cannot claim the balance owed from the shareholders themselves. The shareholders will, at most, lose only the value of their shares.

However, in a small business, lenders, such as banks, often insist on receiving guarantees from shareholders over and above any guarantee from the corporation, particularly if the corporation has few assets of its own. In such instances, the shareholders lose their limited liability regarding those debts.

SHARE STRUCTURE

One advantage with a corporation is income splitting and estate planning. Different classes of shares can be created, leaving the entrepreneur control of the business by retaining the voting shares, and leaving the income generating or capital appreciating shares to others in the family. (See Chapter 11,"Taxes, Canadian and Foreign".)

How shares are allocated among the shareholders, and how the different classes of shares are described (for example, common and preferred shares are described differently) is called the "capital structure" of the company. By allocating different classes and different amounts of shares among the "owners", the company can allocate (i) the risk of loss; (ii) control; (iii) participation in the profits during the existence of the corporation; (iv) distribution of the assets of the corporation upon the liquidation or dissolution of the corporation; and (v) the re-purchase of capital.

Consider the following when issuing more than one class of shares:

- Which class or classes of shares should be voting?
- Should any class be paid its dividends in preference to another?
- Should the dividends for a class be based on a formula, or determined by the directors year-to-year?
- Should dividends be cumulative or non-cumulative (i.e. if dividends are not paid during one year, should they be carried forward to the next, and in preference to others?)
- If the company is dissolved, should one class be paid its value from any remainder in preference to another?
- Should one class of shares be convertible into another class at a set rate within a set time?
- Should the corporation be allowed to redeem shares of a class, at a set price, whether the shareholder wants to or not?

SHAREHOLDER AGREEMENTS

Shareholder agreements range from simple agreements covering only specific corporate matters to general agreements regulating the operation of a corporation in detail. A "unanimous shareholders agreement" is one binding on all the shareholders of the corporation.

Some matters typically included in a shareholders' agreement are:

- Who will be the director(s), officer(s), and auditor(s) of the corporation?
- How the directors and shareholders will vote on certain issues, and what type of contracts and business the corporation will conduct?
- Limiting share transfers to new shareholders. For example, it might allow transfers only if approved by all the shareholders. It might require that those shares first be offered to the remaining shareholders at an arranged price. It might require the remaining shareholders to purchase the shares at an arranged price so that departing shareholder can plan for the value of their shares on retirement or on death. The agreement might also require shareholders to take insurance on each other's death or incapacity, so

that the departing shareholder (or the shareholder's estate) will be fully paid for those shares.

- Requiring arbitration or mediation if there are disputes, thus saving the cost of any court action. It might require a shareholder to transfer shares to the others if the arbitrator concludes that the shareholder has seriously breached the shareholders' agreement.

7

Insurance

Life insurance can be used to pay the following: final bills, the tax on deferred capital gains, foreign taxes, outstanding mortgages, a spousal equalization claim, support for the family, and opportunities (educational and other) for the survivors. Also, many business buy-sell agreements provide for insurance on the owner's interest in the businesses so that the survivor, or the corporation, can purchase the deceased's interest.

Disability insurance funds temporary or permanent loss of employment. It is more expensive for young people, since the probability of becoming disabled exceeds death, especially with improvements in emergency medicine. The financial loss to the family of a disabled wage-earner is often greater than death, since income is lost in both cases, but the disabled person needs to be supported. Almost half of all mortgage foreclosures are due to disability.

Please treat this chapter as just a reminder of the importance of insurance.

LIFE INSURANCE

There are at least three types of life insurance: term, permanent, and universal. However, the industry is constantly changing with new varieties of insurance, often combined with other investment products.

Term insurance is temporary life insurance for a term of usually 1, 5, 10, 15, or 20 years, or "term to 100", with set premiums. Usually, there is an option to renew without additional medical questions or tests, but with higher premiums, until a certain age, often age 70 or 75. Most plans have the right to convert to permanent insurance. For a young person, it is the most affordable protection.

Permanent insurance covers the "whole life" of the insured (not just the term), with guaranteed premium payments until the policy is paid in full. During the early years, the premiums are more than enough to cover the immediate risk, so the extra is invested in "policy reserves". If the insured cancels the contract, the insurance company returns a fair share of the accumulated reserve - this is the "cash surrender value" of the plan.

Universal Life consists of term insurance and an investment account. Because of the investment account, premiums can be increased or decreased, paid when due or at unscheduled dates, or stopped entirely and restarted at the owner's will, provided the policy is adequate.

CAPITAL NEEDS ANALYSIS

The assets available on death should be compared with the amount needed for the survivors - the difference is the insurance required. If a fund is still required after the insured is age 75, then permanent insurance should be considered. The needs analysis should be discussed with a broker or financial adviser, since discounted cash flows and estimated taxes and real rates of return are recommended. After the total needs analysis, later adjustments can be added for single needs, such as a new child, *etc.*

TAXATION OF, AND MATRIMONIAL CLAIMS FOR, INSURANCE PROCEEDS

Insurance proceeds received on the death of the life insured are generally not taxable. (For this reason, the premiums paid for the life insurance are generally not tax deductible.) If a corporation is the beneficiary of a life insurance policy (common in buy-sell agreements in closely held corporations), the corporation may be able to transfer the life insurance proceeds to other shareholders without tax.

Insurance proceeds received by a spouse are not included in "net family property" under the Ontario *Family Law Act* and are not subject to spousal equalization.

The amount payable under an insurance policy owned by a deceased spouse is included in the value of the deceased's estate when determining support, and can be charged with support payments.

DESIGNATING THE BENEFICIARY

If the testator wants the executor to use insurance proceeds to pay estate debts, then the estate should be designated as the beneficiary. If the testator *irrevocably* designates someone to receive the proceeds on death, then, because the proceeds are not within the control of the estate, they are immune from the deceased's creditors. Also, in certain cases, the law protects *revocable* designations to a spouse, child or grandchild from the deceased's creditors (see Chapter 6).

Part II
Planning Considerations

8

Estate Administration

The executor assembles the deceased's assets, pays the debts and administration costs, then distributes what is left to the beneficiaries. The executor has a reasonable time to do so (sometimes called the "executor's year").

In Ontario, if there is a surviving spouse, unless the spouse consents in writing, the executor should not distribute to beneficiaries within six months of death. This is because the surviving spouse has six months to elect whether to take under the Will or by an equalization payment. See Chapter 9, "The Ontario Family Law Act".

If there are ongoing trusts to administer, the executor transfers the trust assets to the trustee(s). (The new trustee could be the executor.) Each trust is then administered according to its own terms, perhaps for many years. For example, suppose the remainder of the estate is to be paid into two separate trusts for two children until age 25. When the executor has paid the debts and has administered the general estate, the executor closes the estate accounts, and pays the balance into two new separate trust accounts. Tax returns are filed separately for each of the estate account and the two ongoing trusts.

PROBATE - WHEN IS IT REQUIRED?

Probate - *proof* of the Will - is a court declaration that the Will is valid. Whether probate is needed depends on the assets to be administered. For example, if the deceased's assets are a life insurance policy payable directly to the surviving spouse, and joint ownership in the home and some joint bank accounts, then probate is not necessary. The insurance and joint assets pass directly to the survivor outside of the Will.

Even if assets do pass through the Will, probate is not always required. For example, a bank may not require probate if the funds on deposit are not large and if an indemnity can be provided.

In Ontario, probating the Will is expensive: Unless the total assets are less than $1,000, the court fees (essentially a form of tax) are 0.5% on the first $50,000 and 1.5% of the excess. So, if the deceased's assets are $200,000, the court fees are $2,500. And then there are legal fees to prepare and file the court documents.

WHEN THERE IS NO WILL

In Ontario, if there is no will, the first $200,000 of the value of the estate goes to the surviving spouse; the balance is then divided among the spouse and children. Portions for children under eighteen will probably be paid into Court.

If no children survive, and if the deceased was not married, the estate goes to the parents, whom failing, the deceased's brothers and sisters.

The Court will appoint an "Administrator" of the estate, or (as it is now called) an "Estate Trustee without a Will". Normally, the Court appoints someone whom the survivors agree is best able to administer the estate. If the survivors cannot agree, then the Court will likely appoint the spouse, whom failing, the surviving child, parent, or sibling.

In most cases, and before being appointed, the Administrator will be required to post a bond with the Court, at twice the estimated value of the estate. (The cost of the bond will be paid out of the estate.)

SETTLING DEBTS

The executor or administrator can be personally liable for debts of the deceased, unless reasonable efforts are made to ascertain and settle them. The *Trustee Act* describes a procedure for advertising for creditors in the local newspaper where the deceased lived or worked.

The executor should also ask the deceased's family and associates whether there are outstanding debts, and should reserve sufficient assets for at least the "executor's year" to pay them.

TAX RETURNS

The executor files the final T1 return for the period from January 1 to the date of death. There may be returns for prior years. There is a T3 trust return for each year of the administration of the estate - from the date of death until the distribution of the estate. And there may be separate T3 trust returns for any ongoing trusts set up from the estate.

The executor can file up to three optional returns for the deceased. Taxes can be reduced because deductions can be claimed more than once, split between returns, or claimed against specific kinds of income.

Separate returns can be filed for:

- Rights or things – amounts that were not paid at the time of death and that, had the person not died, would have been included in his or her income when received. There are rights or things from employment and other sources.
- Activity as a partner or proprietor with a fiscal year that does not begin or end on the same dates as the calendar year. On this return, income is reported for the time from the end of the fiscal period to the date of death. If this optional return is not filed, all the income must be reported on the final return.
- A testamentary trust. This is for income the deceased was receiving as a result of another person's death. The testamentary trust may have a fiscal period that does not begin or end on the same dates as the calendar year.

There may be special elections such as to roll-over RRSP's or RRIF's to a spouse, to transfer capital property to a spouse, for capital reserves, and for charitable donations.

A tax clearance certificate should be obtained from the tax department before distributing the entire estate. The certificate is issued after all returns are filed and assessed and the executor has paid or secured amounts owing. Without a certificate, the executor can be personally liable for outstanding taxes.

The executor should also let the beneficiaries know which of the amounts they receive from the estate are taxable.

THE DUTY OF IMPARTIALITY

Trustees must not favour one beneficiary over another, except as the trust document directs or permits. Where there are succeeding income and capital interests, the trustees must produce a reasonable income without exposing the capital to undue risk.

What if the trust property favours one beneficiary? For example, an investment might produce a generous income, but no capital gain; or a generous capital gain, but no income. What should the trustees do? The answer depends on the settlor's or testator's intention. In an inter-vivos trusts, where the settlor was alive and chose the property that formed the trust, presumably the settlor thought about the issue and intended the trustees to retain the property. However, in a Will, where the testator would not know which assets would form the estate, the trustees have a greater duty to convert to suitable assets.

What about shares in a closely held family company? If the assets of the company are not suitable investments for the trust, the trustees should sell the shares, unless the trust document tells them to do otherwise. If the trust directs them to retain the shares, then they should take steps to control the company and the assets held by the company. For this reason, the trustees become directors of the company, or they appoint their nominees as directors.

ALLOCATING EXPENSES

The trustees must also maintain an even hand when allocating expenses. In the absence of guidance from the settlor or testator, expenses relating to income are charged to the income beneficiary, and the rest are charged to the capital account. Income expenses usually include taxes, insurance, and the maintenance of property, and capital expenses include major repairs and replacement.

TRUSTEE INVESTMENTS

Unless the document states otherwise, the *Trustee Act* sets out the trustees' investment powers. They are those in which a prudent person would invest.

ESTATE ACCOUNTS AND COMPENSATION

Executors prepare statements of the starting assets, receipts, disbursements, and investments. Income and capital accounts are separated, so as to apportion between income and capital beneficiaries (if there are no income beneficiaries, and everything goes to the capital beneficiary, then the separation between income and capital may not be as important).

The executor is entitled to reasonable compensation for the work. What is reasonable depends on the difficulty. As a rule of thumb, the executor is allowed 5% of the value of the estate - 2 ½% of receipts (income and capital), 2 ½ % of disbursements (income and capital), and, if the assets require management over time, an annual management fee of 2/5ths of 1% of the value of the fund.

9

The Ontario Family Law Act

EQUALIZATION OF NET FAMILY PROPERTY

In Ontario, each spouse is entitled to one-half the gain in the couples' net family property accumulated during the marriage.

To calculate net family property, each spouse sums their net assets before the marriage and on dissolution of the marriage; the difference in their net gains is split equally. (Some property is excluded from the calculation, and the matrimonial home is treated specially – see below.)

The *value* of net family property is equalized by a money payment – specific assets are not divided. Courts normally leave it to the paying spouse to decide how to make the payment; if necessary, the court can ensure payment by granting security over a specific asset, or by ordering that a specific asset be transferred.

The *Family Law Act* defines a "spouse" as either a man or woman who is married to someone of the opposite sex. (Courts and the Legislature will likely expand the definition to include common-law or same-sex relationships to be consistent with the *Charter of Rights* - at the time of writing, the law is uncertain in this area.)

A spouse or partner may have additional common-law claims for a constructive trust or compensatory support, if contributions were made to the relationship to an extent not reflected by an equalization of net family property. (See Chapter 6)

Property: What is Included?

"Property" includes any interest, present or future, vested or contingent, in real or personal property. However, the following is specifically excluded:

1. Property, other than a matrimonial home, that was acquired by gift or inheritance from a third person after the date of the marriage.
2. Income from property referred to in paragraph 1, if the donor or testator has expressly stated that it is to be excluded from the spouse's net family property.
3. Damages or a right to damages for personal injuries, nervous shock, mental distress or loss of guidance, care and companionship, or the part of a settlement that represents those damages.
4. Proceeds or a right to proceeds of a policy of life insurance, as defined in the *Insurance Act*, that are payable on the death of the life insured.
5. Property, other than a matrimonial home, into which property referred to in paragraphs 1 to 4 can be traced.
6. Property that the spouses have agreed by a domestic contract is not to be included in the spouse's net family property.

The Matrimonial Home

A spouse must include (and therefore equalize) the value of a matrimonial home owned on the valuation date, but cannot deduct the value of that home if it was owned when they married. This is so that spouses evenly divide the full value of their matrimonial home, and not just the increase in its value during marriage.

However, the wording of the exception has led to several unusual results. For example, the exception doesn't apply if a different home is owned on the date of marriage than at the valuation date. Also, the exclusion applies to the value of the home on the date of marriage, but apparently not to a mortgage on the home on the date of marriage. Since debts at marriage are subtracted from net family property, the effect is to increase the owner's gain in net family property by the amount of the mortgage, without decreasing it by the value of the home.

To illustrate: suppose the husband's net family property is nil, and the wife's only asset is the matrimonial home. She owned it at marriage. At both marriage and the valuation date, it was worth $100,000. When they married, she had a $70,000 mortgage which she paid off during the marriage. A literal interpretation of the Act would find her gain in net family property to be $170,000: $100,000 for the home on the valuation date, plus $70,000 for having paid off the mortgage during the marriage. Therefore, the equalization payment would be $85,000 - considerably more than half the value of the home.

Variation In Payment - Unconscionability

The court may award more or less than half the difference in the spouse's net family properties if the equalization would be "unconscionable".

However, courts rarely exercise the power, and it is limited to the difference in net family properties. For example, a husband might be worth $1 million and have a net family property of $120,000; his wife might be worth $200,000 and have a net family property of $100,000. The difference is $20,000. The ordinary equalization payment would be $10,000 from the husband to the wife. If a court finds this unconscionable, it cannot award the wife more than $20,000, regardless of the disparity in their personal wealth. (However, she may have a claim for support or a constructive trust.)

Timing of Equalization Payment

Each spouse subtracts the value on the date of marriage from the value on the dissolution of marriage. The date of dissolution of marriage (called the "valuation date") is the earlier of:

1. the date when they separated with no reasonable prospect that they will resume cohabitation;
2. the date a divorce is granted;
3. the date the marriage is declared a nullity;
4. the date one of them commences an application based on improvident depletion by the other, and that is later granted;
5. the day before the date when the first of them dies.

Election on Death

The surviving spouse has six months to choose whether to claim his or her share of the increased net family property during the marriage, or what he or she is to receive under the Will (or if there is no Will, what is provided for by intestacy). The two cannot be combined. If the survivor elects an equalization, the will is interpreted as though the survivor had died first. In addition, if he or she receives benefits from the deceased's insurance policies or pension plans, those benefits are credited against the equalization payment. If the benefits received by the spouse exceed the equalization payment, the estate can demand the excess, unless there is a written designation by the deceased that the payments are to be in addition to equalization.

As noted above, the valuation date is the day before death (unless the spouses were already separated). Therefore, the cash value of a life insurance policy and an interest in property held jointly with others, including the spouse, are included in the deceased's net family property. This applies even though these two assets may pass to the spouse independently of the will or a family property claim.

A deceased's net family property is reduced by capital gains taxes payable as a result of the deemed disposition on death.

Planning for a Spouse's Election on Death

Careful planning is required if the surviving spouse is not to receive the whole estate, since the survivor could choose an equalization payment. For example, if the Will leaves the survivor income from a trust, the present value of that income may be less than the equalization amount. Or, perhaps the spouse will simply prefer an outright equalization payment rather than trust income. Planning the estate is difficult, since the value of assets left to the spouse may change by the time of death.

One way to preserve the plan intact is to have life insurance to fund an equalization claim.

If the survivor elects equalization instead of what is given under the will, the survivor's benefits under the will are eliminated (unless the will says otherwise) and the interests of the other beneficiaries are advanced. What effect does this have on the estate plan? The spousal rollover may not be available - how does this change the tax situation? The interests of the other beneficiaries will be accelerated - does this create any special problems? The testator may want to specify which bequests will bear the burden of the equalization payment. Finally, the testator may still want the spouse to act as an executor or as the trustee of a testamentary trust, or to receive something under the will. If so, it should be expressly stated in the will that the entitlement applies even if the spouse elects against the will.

The testator can reduce net family property by giving property away before death - by outright gifts, by gifts to trusts, by restructuring corporate securities. However, this raises the possibility of a claim for improvident depletion by the spouse before death, and a *Fraudulent Conveyances Act* action after death.

A spouse can sever the joint tenancy of property held jointly with his or her spouse. This can be done unilaterally, by registering a deed The interest in the property will be included in net family property, but it will pass through the deceased's estate, instead of directly to the joint owner.

Many couples make marriage contracts to waive equalization. Some are older couples who were married before and have their own assets and children, and they want to leave what they have to their own children. Many do not want to deal with matrimonial litigation while grieving the death of their spouse. See Chapter 16 for an example.

Dependants

The Court can order the estate to make adequate provision for a dependant - see s. 58(1) of the Ontario *Succession Law Reform Act*. A dependant is:

- the deceased's spouse, including someone the deceased cohabited with continuously for at least three years, or with whom he or she was in a relationship of some permanence if they were the natural or adoptive parents of a child;
- the deceased's parent, including a grandparent, or someone who treated the deceased as a child of his or her family;
- the deceased's child, including an illegitimate or adopted child, a grandchild, or someone the deceased treated as a child of the family; or
- the deceased's brother or sister.

The deceased must have been providing (or legally should have been providing) support to the dependant prior to death. The amount of support is based on the need of the dependant and the ability of the estate to pay.

The Court can order the estate to pay a lump sum, or ongoing payments, or that specific property be transferred to the dependant, either outright, in trust, for life, for a period of time, or as security for the payment of support.

A claim for support is often combined with a challenge to the testator's capacity, because a failure to make adequate provision for dependants shows an inappreciation of the moral claims upon the estate. In determining capacity, section 62(3) provides that "the court may accept such evidence as it considers proper of the deceased's reasons, so far as ascertainable, for making the dispositions in his or her will, or for not making adequate provision for a dependant, as the case may be, including any statement in writing signed by the deceased."

The testator can make a statement explaining why someone is not to be supported. The statement should indicate that the testator has made other arrangements for support, such as pre-death gifts, or designating the claimant as the recipient of the proceeds of insurance policies and RRSP and pension plans.

Avoiding Equalization Claims When Giving to a Child

A parent who is giving to a child, may wish to limit an equalization claim by the spouse of the child. A simple solution for a lifetime gift is to give nothing - make a loan instead. If the loan is properly documented, it will be deducted from the child's net family property at marriage and at the valuation date. However, loans to family members may cause tax attribution.

A parent may wish to exclude the income on the gift to the child. As noted above, specific exclusions to property include: "property, other than a matrimonial home, that was acquired by gift or inheritance after the date of the marriage, and income from such property if the donor expressly stated that the income is to be excluded."

If the parent gives the child an interest in a family corporation, don't have the child subscribe and pay for the shares - the gift exclusion will be lost. Instead, have shares issued to the parents and then given to the child.

Another solution is to ask the child, and his or her spouse, to do a marriage contract excluding the gift or inheritance, and the income on it, from an equalization claim.

10

Incapacity

For the sick and elderly, incapacity is not a hypothetical - it looms around the corner; it concerns and interferes with daily life. Decisions can be made one day, but not the next. Choices may be understood, without the desire or energy to act.

There are two concerns: First, who will manage the assets and finances on incapacity? Second, who will make decisions about personal care and medical treatment?

Sadly, many people know what should happen; they know who should act, but they procrastinate and leave matters disorganized, complicated; and then their "substitute decision maker" can't make the right decisions, or can't make them at the right time.

FINANCIAL DECISIONS

In Ontario, under the *Substitute Decisions Act, 1992*, when someone is found incapable, the Public Guardian and Trustee ("PGT") temporarily becomes their guardian of property. If there is a continuing power of attorney for property (see Chapter 4), the PGT is automatically replaced as soon as the attorney files a copy of the document with the PGT, along with an undertaking to act in accordance with the continuing power of attorney.

If there is no continuing power of attorney over all the person's property, the PGT continues as the guardian of property and manages the person's finances until another suitable person can assume the role. The following persons may apply to the PGT to replace the PGT as the guardian of property:

1. The incapable person's spouse or partner;
2. A relative of the incapable person;

3. The incapable person's attorney under a continuing power of attorney, if the power of attorney was made before the certificate of incapacity was issued and does not give the attorney authority over all of the incapable person's property;
4. A trust corporation within the meaning of the *Loan and Trust Corporations Act*, if the incapable person's spouse or partner consents in writing to the application.

The applicant must file a management plan with the PGT. The PGT shall consider the incapable person's current wishes, if they can be ascertained, the closeness of the applicant's relationship to the person, whether the management plan is appropriate, and whether the applicant is suitable to manage the property. The PGT may require the applicant to post security.

If the PGT refuses the appointment, reasons must be given in writing. If the applicant disputes the refusal of the PGT in writing, the PGT must then apply to the Ontario Court (General Division) to decide whether the applicant should replace the PGT.

The guardian of property must act in the person's best interests and in accordance with the management plan filed with the PGT, and has the same duties and is entitled to the same compensation as an attorney for property (see Chapter 2). Expenditures must be reasonably necessary for the person's support, education and care, or for the person's dependants, in accordance with their accustomed standard of living, or to meet other legal obligations.

Temporary Guardian of Property

If, after an investigation, the PGT has reasonable grounds to believe that a person is incapable of managing property and that the prompt appointment of a temporary guardian of property is required to prevent "serious adverse effects", the PGT shall apply to the court for an order appointing the PGT as temporary guardian of property for a period up to 90 days. " Serious adverse effects" is defined in the statute as: "Loss of a significant part of a person's property, or a person's failure to provide necessities of life for himself or herself or for dependants." The Court order may grant the PGT all or just specific powers, and it may suspend the powers of an attorney under a continuing power of attorney during the term of the temporary guardianship.

How is Someone Found Incapable of Managing Property?

Someone is found incapable of managing property if they have been admitted to a psychiatric facility or if they have been assessed incapable by a government designated "assessor".

Anyone, perhaps a concerned neighbour or a family member, may request an assessment of a person's capacity. No assessment shall be performed unless the request is in the prescribed form and states that,

1. the person requesting the assessment has reason to believe that the other person may be incapable of managing property;
2. the person requesting the assessment has made reasonable inquiries and has no knowledge of the existence of any attorney under a continuing power of attorney that gives the attorney authority over all of the other person's property; and
3. the person requesting the assessment has made reasonable inquiries and has no knowledge of any spouse, partner or relative of the other person who intends to make an application for the appointment of a guardian of property for the other person.

The government designated assessor will advise the person of the purpose and legal significance of the assessment, then interview the person, then speak to those who know and have been communicating with the person, and then determine whether they are capable of managing their property.

The person can refuse to be assessed. If, however, there are reasonable grounds to believe that the person is incapable, then an application to court (on notice to the person) can be made for an assessment and, if necessary, the court will order the assessment; in some cases, the person may be detained for the assessment.

Under the *Mental Health Act*, if either a physician, a police officer in an urgent situation, or a Justice of the Peace from information upon oath, is of the opinion that a person is apparently suffering from mental disorder of a nature or quality that likely will result in, serious bodily harm to the person, serious bodily harm to another person, or imminent and serious physical impairment of the person, he or she can be compelled for a psychiatric assessment and can be detained for up to 72 hours. If the mental disorder and the potential harm is confirmed on the assessment, the person may be detained at a psychiatric facility and, as mentioned above, the person will then be considered incapable of managing property.

PERSONAL CARE DECISIONS

"Personal care" decisions include: medical treatment decisions, decisions about admissions to nursing homes and care facilities; decisions about nutrition and hygiene; decisions about safety; decisions about clothing and recreation; and decisions about social services provided to the person.

When someone becomes incapable of making these decisions, a "substitute decision maker" steps forward. The attorney for personal care is the substitute decision maker (see Chapter 3), unless replaced by a court appointed guardian of the person.

Anyone may apply to court to be appointed the guardian of the person, but the application will be denied if the personal care decisions can be made without declaring the person incapable. The PGT will not be appointed the guardian, unless there is no other suitable person available and willing to be appointed guardian. The court may limit the guardianship to a particular time period or impose other conditions.

The guardian of the person will be chosen depending on: whether the proposed guardian is the attorney under a continuing power of attorney for property; the incapable person's current wishes, if they can be ascertained; and the closeness of the applicant's personal relationship to the incapable person.

The guardian of the person has similar duties as the attorney for personal care (see Chapter 3). The guardian should explain to the incapable person the guardian's powers and duties, and must follow the person's wishes. If the person's wishes have not or cannot be expressed, then according to their best interests, including the values and beliefs the person would act on if capable. The guardian should choose the least restrictive and intrusive course of action that is available and appropriate.

The guardian should, as far as possible, foster the person's independence, and should encourage the person to participate, to the best of his or her abilities, in the decisions made. The guardian should also foster regular personal contact between the person and their supportive family and friends.

Medical Treatment Decisions and Admissions to a Care Facility

Medical treatment decisions and admissions to a care facility are governed by the Ontario *Health Care Consent Act*. No treatment can be undertaken without the informed consent of the patient or, if the patient is incapable, the informed consent of the "substitute decision maker", unless it is an emergency and an informed consent cannot be obtained. Similarly, no one can be admitted to a nursing home or care facility, and no one is to receive a personal assistance service, without their informed consent, or the informed consent of their substitute decision maker, unless it is a crisis and an informed consent cannot be obtained. For medical treatment and admissions to care facilities, the substitute decision maker is in this order of priority:

1. The incapable person's court appointed guardian of the person, if the guardian has authority to give or refuse consent to the treatment.
2. The incapable person's attorney for personal care, if the power of attorney confers authority to give or refuse consent to the treatment.
3. The incapable person's representative appointed by the *Consent and Capacity Review Board*, if the representative has authority to give or refuse consent to the treatment.
4. The incapable person's spouse or partner.
5. A child or parent of the incapable person, or a children's aid society or other person who is lawfully entitled to give or refuse consent to the treatment in the place of the parent. This paragraph does not include a parent who has only a right of access. If a children's aid society or other person is lawfully entitled to give or refuse consent to the treatment in the place of the parent, this paragraph does not include the parent.
6. A parent of the incapable person who has only a right of access.
7. A brother or sister of the incapable person.
8. Any other relative of the incapable person.
9. The Public Guardian and Trustee.

The patient's physician or health practitioner is not listed as a substitute decision maker. Even if the health practitioner receives a copy of the power of attorney or "living will" and is aware of the person's general attitude to treatment, an informed consent to the specific treatment is still required (from the person or their substitute decision maker), unless it is an emergency and a consent cannot be obtained. If it is an emergency, then the health practitioner follows the last known wishes of the patient, but the treatment may be continued for only so long as is reasonably necessary to obtain a consent for the continuation of the treatment. Therefor treatment choices should be discussed in advance with those who will make the personal care decisions.

The substitute decision maker must follow the person's wishes, if the wishes are known. If the wishes are not known, or if it is impossible to comply with the wishes, then in accordance with the person's values, beliefs and best interests. If the person's expressed wishes are old, and the substitute decision maker believes that the treatment or care facility is significantly better now than would have been anticipated when the wish was expressed, an application can be made to the *Consent and Capacity Review Board* to consent to the treatment or admission.

When is Someone Incapable of Making Personal Care Decisions?

If there is an attorney for personal care, the attorney shall make decisions if:

1. For medical treatment decisions, the person is "not able to understand the information that is relevant to making a decision about the treatment, admission or personal assistance service, as the case may be, and is not able to appreciate the reasonably foreseeable consequences of a decision or lack of decision."
2. For all other decisions, there are reasonable grounds to believe that the grantor is incapable of making the decision. In addition, a power of attorney can require an independent assessment of capacity before the attorney can make decisions.

If there is no attorney for personal care, and if a neighbour or family member is concerned about someone's capacity for personal decisions, an application to court to appoint a guardian of the person is required. (There is no mechanism for a preliminary assessment before a court application, as is the case for property decisions.) Evidence of the incapacity (such as a physician's findings and evidence of inappropriate behaviour by family and friends) should be gathered, and a management plan provided, as part of the court application.

If the person is suffering "serious adverse effects", such as "serious illness or injury, or deprivation of liberty or personal security", then the PGT shall investigate and, if there are reasonable grounds, the PGT shall apply to the court to become their temporary guardian of the person for a maximum of 90 days.

PLANNING FOR INCAPACITY

General Concerns

There are several things that can be done. The choice, and the combination, will vary with the circumstances.

What is the nature of the possible incapacity? Is the illness cyclical, permanent, or terminal? Will the person completely lose the ability to communicate? Is he or she likely to deny the incapacity? Does the person need to be protected from their own actions during the incapacity?

What about the family? Do they want to control the affairs during the incapacity?

What are the person's obligations? Are there dependants? Are there gifts to charities or others that they wish to continue during the incapacity?

Who can manage the estate? Will it need special expertise or professional management?

These are some of the possible arrangements, from the least to the greatest delegation of authority.

Joint Bank Accounts

A bank account, held jointly as a convenience, is a simple way to deal with cash. The other joint account holder can pay the person's bills and deposit cheques without an endorsement. Both account holders have access to the account, before and during the person's incapacity.

Putting money into a joint account may raise questions of title to the account. If the joint holders are spouses, they will be presumed to own the money equally. Otherwise, the rules of resulting trust will apply (see Chapter 1). If this is a concern, a power of attorney over the account is better.

Agency Arrangements

Trust companies, investment dealers, and investment counsel are in the business of managing assets. Investment dealers and investment counsel manage investment portfolios; trust companies manage all property. The arrangements can vary from a fully discretionary account where the agent decides what investments to buy and sell and when to do so, to an arrangement where the client makes the decisions and the agent simply carries them out. In either case, the client and the agent can arrange that the agent will collect the income, invest surplus cash, remit funds to the client, pay bills for the client, file tax returns, and do anything else that may be wanted. The fees vary with the work done. This is often a useful arrangement. Again, the forms should contain the terms of the arrangement, including provision for the principal's incapacity.

Powers of Attorney

See Chapter 2 for continuing power of attorney for property, and Chapter 3 for the power of attorney for personal care.

Inter-Vivos Trusts

See Chapter 1 on trusts.

Before death or incapacity, an owner may want trustees to manage the asset and to distribute it according to a plan. The plan may be to use the asset for the spouse, or for someone else, and then for another person. It may need special management. By forming the trust before incapacity, the owner can see that the plan will operate effectively and not lose value later. And, on death, the estate will be easier to administer because the plan will already have been set-up.

The owner can be the trustee, or one of the trustees. A power of appointment can be given to someone else. The document should provide for the succession of management as well as for the interests of the beneficiaries. There may be tax considerations, but these can usually be overcome.

11

Taxes, Canadian and Foreign

CANADIAN INCOME TAXES

Tax planning is part of estate planning. The purpose is to not pay tax prematurely, and to not pay unnecessary tax.

In Canada, there are no estate taxes or death duties, federal or provincial. Instead, there are "deemed" dispositions of assets on death, with the result that previously untaxed income and capital gains are taxed at death. There are, of course, many other taxes - goods and services tax, sales tax, property tax, tax on transactions (such as land transfer tax), court costs on probating wills - but this chapter refers only to Canadian income tax and, briefly, foreign estate taxes.

This chapter is intended only as a reminder of some estate-planning considerations. The subject is far too complex for a detailed review in this book. Tax law changes too often to be able to write comprehensively about tax in this form.

Do not rely on this chapter for deciding about the tax consequences of a proposed step. If these points remind you of a tax consideration, please go to the usual authorities for a more complete and up-to-date review.

The following are points that often are considered. Generally, they involve these questions: What will the tax be? Does it have to be paid, or is there an exemption? When does it have to be paid? Who, of the beneficiaries, will pay it?

WHO IS TAXED?

- individuals;
- corporations;
- trusts, testamentary and inter-vivos.

WHAT IS TAXED?

- income: income is what is received for labour or services; and rent, interest, dividends and the like from investments.
- capital gains: a capital gain is the difference between the tax-cost and the proceeds of disposition of the capital property, after various adjustments.

TAXING THE INDIVIDUAL

Estate planning matters include the principal residence exemption from capital gains tax, tax deferral plans, spreading income among the family so that the lowest overall tax is paid.

The home - The Principal Residence Exemption

- The capital gain on a principal residence is exempt from gains tax. It can be a house, condominium, cottage, farm house with about one acre of land, or shares in a co-operative housing unit, in Canada or elsewhere.
- The taxpayer must live in the residence.
- A person can only have one principal residence each year. Before 1982, each spouse could own a residence and each could claim the exemption. Since 1982, a couple and their unmarried children under 18 can have only one principal residence among them.

Pensions, RRSP's, and Deferred Savings Plans

- If a portion of earned income is placed in registered plan with approved investments, then the investment, and its growth and income earned in the plan, will not be taxed until funds are withdrawn.
- The portion of earned income that can go into a plan is confined to a stated limit.
- All amounts withdrawn will be taxed as income.
- Taxpayers can designate those who will receive the death benefits when they die by making designations in their plans or in their Wills.

Attribution and The Family

- Income splitting means dividing pre-tax income among family members to reduce the total tax paid on the income. Income taxes are "progressive"; rates increase as income increases.
- Income is "attributed" back to the member of the family who transfers the property to another member. While the transfer carries with it the income to the property transferred, the transferor pays the tax on the income on that property, not the transferee. This is too complex a subject to discuss in detail in this book, but includes transfers to a common-law spouse, and to some family trusts and corporations, and some interest-free or low-interest loans made to someone who is not at "arm's length".
- With some exceptions, non-arm's length transfers of capital property, including a gift or inheritance, are deemed to occur at fair market value. The transferor pays tax on the capital gains up to the date of transfer; the transferee pays any capital gains tax from that date forward.
- However, unless fair market value is actually paid by the transferee-spouse, transfers between spouses do not take place at fair market value. When the transferee-spouse sells the asset, the full capital gains based on the original tax-cost.
- Exceptions to the attribution rules include the following:
  - Business income.
  - Income on income.
  - Contributions to a spouse's RRSP if the contributions are not withdrawn from the plan within two calendar years.

THE SMALL CORPORATION

- For small business corporations that qualify, the lower than usual rate on the first $200,000 of income applies. The reduction does not eliminate the tax, it only defers it. When the corporation pays a dividend to its shareholder, it pays a "distribution tax" which brings the total tax paid back to the ordinary corporate level.
- Tax "integration" tends to equalize the total tax paid by business owners whether, to operate the business, they incorporate or use a proprietorship.
- Canadian private corporations pay a refundable tax on dividend income. Inter-corporate dividends between connected private

corporations are not subject to that tax. The tax is refunded when the corporation pays the dividend to the shareholder.

- When a corporation redeems or purchases its shares, instead of the shareholder receiving a gain if the redemption or purchase price exceeds the tax-cost, the shareholder receives a "deemed" dividend of the excess of the price over the paid-up capital of the shares.
- Dividends paid out the corporation's "capital dividend account" are tax-free to the shareholder. The capital dividend account includes the untaxed 25% of capital gains in the corporation, and most proceeds of insurance owned by the corporation on the life of a principal.
- Most loans to shareholders are included in the shareholder's income, unless the shareholder repays the entire amount before the end of the corporation's next tax year.
- Start-up losses that are incurred before incorporation are not normally deductible against post-incorporation profits.

TAXING THE TRUST

- Trusts pay tax and file returns as though they were separate taxpayers.
- Trusts are either residents or non-residents of Canada. Different tax considerations apply to each. The residence of a trust is generally where the managing trustee or the majority of trustees reside.
- There are two types of trusts: testamentary and inter-vivos. A testamentary trust is a trust arising because of an individual's death. An inter-vivos trust is any other trust.
- The testamentary trust is taxed at the graduated personal rates. The inter-vivos trust is taxed at the highest marginal rate. The testamentary trust can choose a year-end that is any time within twelve months of the deceased's death; the inter-vivos trust's tax-year must be the calendar year.

Calculation and Flow-through of Income

- A trust calculates its income in the same way as an individual. The trustee reports the taxable income, deducts the income that is paid or payable to the beneficiaries, and pays tax on the remainder. However, unlike an individual, the trust cannot claim the personal tax credits.

- The beneficiaries include the income received or receivable from a trust in their tax returns for the calendar year in which the trust's fiscal year ends. For a testamentary trust, this allows the tax to be deferred for a year.
- Certain kinds of income from a trust can retain their character when paid to the beneficiaries who live in Canada, including taxable dividends, capital gains, foreign income, superannuation and pension benefits.
- Assets transferred to beneficiaries to pay their right to capital in the trust are treated as "rollovers", that is the assets transfer and are received by the beneficiaries at the trust's tax-cost. Assets transferred to pay their right to income are not treated as rollovers.
- In some circumstances, some trusts are deemed to dispose of and immediately re-acquire all their capital assets at fair market value every 21 years. Depreciable property is treated disposed of at the midway between their fair market value and their undepreciated capital cost.
- Most amounts paid or payable to non-resident beneficiaries are subject to withholding tax. Also, income such as net taxable gains and taxable dividends, cannot retain their character when paid to non-resident beneficiaries.

CAPITAL GAINS AND ROLLOVERS

Normally, transfers of capital assets between individuals, companies or trusts attracts capital gains tax on the difference between the fair market proceeds of distribution and the tax-cost.

Capital Gains Exemption - Family Farms and Small Business Corporation Shares

Every individual (but not a trust or corporation) resident in Canada is entitled to a lifetime "capital gains exemption" of up to $500,000 on farm property and on shares of qualifyiing small business corporations. (The general $100,000 capital gains exemption for all kinds of property was eliminated as of February 22, 1994.).

To qualify for the farm property exemption:

- The property must be used for farming by a member of the family either in the year it is sold; the owner has owned it for at a stated time, used it for farming on a regular and continuous basis, and have earned more gross income from farming than from other sources.
- The same rules apply to shares of a family farm corporation or an interest in a family farm partnership.

To qualify for the exemption on shares of a small business corporation:

- The corporation must use, and for stated time must have used, substantially all of its assets carrying on an active business in Canada, or own shares or debt in other companies which do.
- The individual (or a person related to the individual) must have held the shares in the corporation for a stated time before selling them.

Capital Gains on Death

- All the testator's capital assets are deemed sold immediately before death.
- The executor files a final T1 return for the taxpayer for the period from January 1 to the date of death. This return includes the capital gains on those deemed sales as well as the deceased's regular income during the portion of the year.
- Estate planning matter: In most Wills, taxes are included in the deceased's debts to be paid out of the remainder of the estate rather than out of specific bequests. If an asset with accrued and untaxed gains (or other) tax is specifically given, unless the Will says otherwise, the beneficiary of that gift will not pay the tax on the asset, the beneficiaries of the remainder will. This is the common question: "Who pays the tax?" The answer is part of the estate plan, to be included in the Will.

Rollovers

- In certain circumstances, property can be transferred from the deceased to beneficiaries on a "rollover" basis, that is, at the deceased's tax-cost. No gain will occur until the beneficiary disposes of the property.

- Rollovers are available for property left to the deceased's spouse or to a trust for the spouse, for farm property left to the deceased's children, and, depending on the circumstances, for RRSP's left to the spouse and children.
- Estate planning matter. This is part of the above question: "Who pays the tax?" The testator can make the choice of whether or not to use a rollover for a particular asset, or it can be left to the executor and beneficiary. If it is possible to use an exemption instead of a rollover, use the exemption - a rollover only defers the tax; an exemption completely eliminates it. In any case, the Will should leave clear instructions.

Spouses and "Qualifying Spousal Trusts"

- Transfers to the deceased's spouse, or to a "qualifying spouse trust", can be rolled over at no tax cost. Both the deceased and the spouse must have been Canadian residents immediately before the death. A qualifying spouse trust must entitle the spouse to all the trust's income that arises before the spouse's death, and only the spouse may receive or use any of the trust's income or capital before the spouse's death. Also, the property for the trust must vest indefeasibly in the trust within 36 months of the testator's death, and the trust must be a Canadian resident when the property vests.
- The rollover is also available for inter-vivos transfers between spouses and spousal trusts.

The Family Farm

- Farm property can be rolled over to the child, grandchild or great-grandchild provided the transferor (or spouse or one of their children) has used the property "principally" in a farming business, and provided the transferor (or spouse or one of their children) has actively engaged in farming on a regular and continuous basis.

Registered Retirement Savings Plans

- Ordinarily, the final return to the date of death for a deceased taxpayer includes the fair market value of all the property in the RRSP as though the deceased collapsed the RRSP immediately before death. The entire value is included as income, not as a capital gain; none of the other rollovers or exemptions are available and the full amount is taxable.

- However, if the taxpayer names the spouse as the beneficiary of the plan, the spouse is deemed to receive the plan benefits. If the RRSP has not matured, the receipt is a "refund of premiums", and the spouse can transfer the entire amount into the spouse's RRSP. In effect, the RRSP is rolled over tax-free. If the RRSP is left to the spouse through the deceased's will, the executor and the spouse can file a joint election that achieves the same result. In certain circumstances, a deceased taxpayer's RRSP receipt can be rolled over to a dependant child or grandchild.
- Estate planning matter: Another "Who pays the tax?" consideration. Spouses (for example, second spouses) who receive RRSP benefits and transfer them to their own plans pay the tax, as income, on what they withdraw as they do so. As between spouses and other beneficiaries, the Will can say who receives, and who pays the tax on, the RRSP benefits.

Reserves and Other Deferrals

- A reserve is a deferral of capital gains tax. It is available if part of the sale proceeds of capital property are not due until a later tax year.
- A special deferral is available to an estate. The executor can elect to pay all or part of the tax on deemed at-death asset dispositions in ten equal consecutive annual instalments, with interest and security.

ESTATE FREEZING

Owners can "freeze" the value of their growth-potential assets so that the future growth passes to their spouses or children. The increase in asset value up to the freeze date is taxed in the hands of the taxpayer. Later growth is taxed in the hands of the spouse or children.

Gifting

- A simple method is a gift. Because the gift is deemed made at fair market value, the capital gain up to the date of the gift is taxed to the donor. Later growth is taxed to the gift-recipient.

- The attribution rules will apply. On gifts to minor children, the income, but not future capital gains, is attributed back to the parent.
- A parent can retain control of the asset by making the gift to a trust that the parent manages for the children. Or, if the assets are the shares of a private corporation, the parent can retain voting control.
- Estate planning matter: The donor may want to protect the child against claims by the child's spouse. Under the *Family Law Act* (Ontario), if the child is married, the value of the gift will be excluded from the child's net family property and; in addition, the donor can choose to exclude later earnings on the gift.

Direct Sale

The same considerations as a gift to the child apply, except:

- There will be no attribution if the transaction is at fair market value.
- Estate planning matter: Under the *Family Law Act* (Ontario), the net family property exclusion that applies to a gift does not apply to a sale; the married child must include the property.
- Estate planning matter: Taking back a promissory note can defer the parent's capital gain on the sale. Reserves can be claimed to spread the gain over a maximum of five years. The parent can forgive the note in the Will; if not, the child could buy insurance on the parent's life to pay for the balance owing on the parent's death.

Estate Freezing With a Corporation

By using several classes of shares, the owner, with voting shares, can retain control of the business, and transfer future income and capital growth to other family members. Shares held for children can be held in trust.

The transfer of assets to a corporation is deemed to be at fair market value. Like a gift or a sale, this would attract the tax on the accrued gain. However, this tax can be deferred by the "section 85" or "section 86" rollover.

The Section 85 Rollover

- The transferor transfers the asset to the corporation and receives preferred shares. The transferor and the corporation can elect to have the transaction take place at an "elected price" that is between the transferor's tax-cost of the asset and its fair market value. The elected price is deemed to be the corporation's cost base of the asset, as well as the transferor's cost base of the preferred shares received by the transferor for the asset.
- This raises the possibility of double tax. If the corporation sells the asset and if the transferor sells his or her preferred shares, the capital gain that accrued before the freeze will be taxed twice. This would also happen if the deceased died. To alleviate this, the *Tax Act* allows en election to eliminate the tax on the preferred shares on a deemed disposition on death if the corporation redeems the preferred shares within one year of the death.
- The transferor is permitted to receive consideration that is part preferred shares and part other consideration. The total consideration must not be more than the asset's fair market value. The shares can be issued for the full price; or the non-share consideration can be up to the amount of the election.
- The corporation must be a taxable Canadian corporation.
- The consideration received by the transferor must include at least one share.
- Only certain property can be frozen, including depreciable and non-depreciable capital property, eligible capital property, resource property, and inventory other than real estate. It does not include real estate inventory and any real estate owned by a non-resident of Canada.

The Internal Section 86 Freeze

An "internal freeze" involves a reorganization of an existing corporation. Usually, the transferor owns common shares of a corporation, and wants to give the children the future growth in the corporation. To do this, the corporation converts the transferor's common shares into fixed-value preferred shares and the children are issued common shares. Any capital gain is deferred until the parent disposes the new shares. The corporation can also give the transferor non-share consideration, such as cash or a promissory note.

FOREIGN TAXES, ESTATE TAXES

Most countries outside Canada tax the at-death transfer of wealth through estate taxes and death duties.

There are two concerns regarding foreign assets. Firstly, which law applies to the disposition or succession of the property - the foreign or Canadian law? Secondly, what are the taxes, and will the other country impose withholding taxes?

WHICH LAW APPLIES?

In general, for land ("immoveables"), it is the law of the location of the land that governs its disposition or succession. For all other property ("moveables"), it is the law of the domicile of the transferor. So, for example, if a testator resides in Canada, owns a condominium in Florida, common shares in a Texas oil corporation, and a home in Canada, then: (1) the law of Florida governs the succession of the Florida condominium, including whether there are spousal or dependant claims on the land; (2) the law of Ontario applies to the Texas shares, because they are "moveables"; and (3) Ontario law applies to the Toronto home and its succession and claims by the spouse and dependants.

The law of the jurisdiction where the land is located may import aspects of the law of the domicile.

US Tax on Income from US Assets

US source income is subject to US tax, even if the person is not a US resident. There are withholding taxes on rental income, dividends from US companies, sales of shares of US companies, sales of US real estate, and other properties. The non-resident files a US tax return, and is credited for the amount withheld on the sale. The Canada-US tax treaty may provide a credit against Canadian tax for the US tax ultimately paid.

Canadians who reside in the US for more than a stated time, for US tax purposes, may become US residents.

US Estate Tax

US federal and state estate taxes apply to persons who do not reside in the US and who have assets in the US. The federal tax computes the gross fair market value of all the deceased's property in the US, less certain allowable deductions. Once the "taxable estate" is determined, US federal estate tax applies at graduated rates.

The following assets are subject to US estate tax:

- real estate located in the US;
- certain tangible personal property located in the US;
- shares of US corporations regardless of the location of the certificates or where they trade;
- debts of US persons, including bonds from governments;
- interests in partnerships carrying on business in the US.

The following US-located assets are normally excluded:

- shares of a non-US corporations (regardless of the location of the share certificates and the location of the corporation's assets);
- US bank deposits;
- certain US corporate bonds publicly traded outside the US or that are targeted to non-US buyers;
- life insurance proceeds payable on the death of a non-US decedent.

Canadian Credit for Foreign Estate Taxes

On death, Canada taxes accrued capital gains on all property, including gains on foreign property. Under tax treaties, some credits are available for the foreign-paid estate taxes and death duties.

Part III
Example Situations

12

The Young Family

Cindy and Keith are in their late thirties, with two primary school age children. Both have been working in middle management for five years since graduating from university; they have a house in the suburbs with a high ratio mortgage; employment pension plans worth "something"; she has life insurance through employment of $100,000 and his is $75,000. Their employment disability plans are minimal. They each have about $5,000 in RRSP mutual funds; and, of course, the minivan.

They come to you for their "wills". They've heard something about powers of attorney. They each want to leave everything to the survivor, whom failing, to the children. (In private, one politely wonders what happens if the other remarries some years after death - what happens to the kids' share?). They want "simple" wills and, being parsimonious, they ask for a quote.

THEIR REAL CONCERNS

- What's going to happen to the kids if we both die in a car crash?
- How can we reduce taxes?

DECISIONS TO BE MADE

- Who should be the guardian of the children if both die? Should the same person be guardian of their property? (It's simplier if one person is both.)
- Are they aware that the appointment might only last for 90 days, and could be subject to the "best interests of the children" as determined by a court?
- Who should be the executor if both die? Do they want an alternate executor, if their first choice is unable or unwilling to act? Do they know that their executor need not be an "expert"? (The executor can obtain legal or tax advice.)
- Should the executor have the power to sell the house and all assets, or must the executor preserve certain assets for a time? (Probably not a good idea to bind the executor too much, since circumstances may change.)
- Should the fund for the children be pooled together, or held and invested separately? (Unless they expect a significant estate for the children with different trustees of the funds, it makes sense to pool the children's fund.)
- At what age should the children receive their share? Should the trustee of the fund(s) have the power to encroach on capital in the meantime?
- Is the house presently owned as joint tenants, tenants in common, or is it registered in one name solely? (If held jointly, the house automatically goes to survivor of them outside of the will, thus saving probate fees.)
- Are the other assets, including bank accounts, held jointly?
- Is the survivor the designated beneficiary of the life insurance plans? (Probably a good idea, to protect from creditors and probate fees.) What about the RRSPs?
- Assuming that they may not revise their wills for a long time, if one of their children dies before them leaving a child or children, do they want those grandchildren to receive the deceased child's share? (Per stirpes? Per capita?)
- Do they wish to leave anything to a charity, to friends, or to other family?
- Is there a marriage or separation agreement affecting their estate?

- Let them know that the survivor, whatever they may receive under the will, can elect the survivor's equalization payment. Also, the survivor must continue to support the children.
- Let them know what powers of attorney are, and let them know that, statistically, it is far more likely that one or both of them becomes disabled, rather then die. So powers of attorney are a good idea.
- Suggest that they review their life insurance.

See the sample will for a young couple in Chapter 17.

13

The Second Marriage

The second marriage we discuss here is by persons in their fifties and older. They may have been divorced or their spouses have died. Both have adult children. Each has accumulated some net worth; this may include a home, a cottage. They may simply live together, or they may marry. One may support the other, or not.

Their children may or may not get along with the partner, and with the other's children. Unless there is careful planning, it is probable that differences will be aggravated when one of them dies. Usually, children do not like it when their family assets go to another family, instead of to them.

They should deal with these issues, and review them over the years.

The following illustrates some of these questions.

A SAMPLE SITUATION

Peter and Florence are to be married. He's sixty-one and she's fifty-five. He has three children, all in their thirties. She has two sons, ages seventeen and twenty-one. Peter is a professional engineer; Florence is a school principal.

His wife died of cancer four years ago. It was hard. She had chemotherapy and radiation. He knows the frailties of life, the grieving, the depression, and the loneliness. His daughter stayed with him during this time, but she's thirty-one now, doing a Masters in another town, moving on with her life.

Florence's husband left her with the boys ten years ago. She buried herself in work, becoming principal, organizing school activities, and is now chief negotiator at the school board. The older boy is studying pre-law in university; the younger, Larry, was recently diagnosed as a mild schizophrenic; he's always been difficult, she used to blame it on the marriage breakup, but he isn't improving; she worries about him.

Each has a house that is mortgage-free; a pension plan, life insurance, disability and health insurance through work; some RRSP's; a portfolio of securities outside their RRSP's, and small operating bank accounts. Florence will inherit from her parents.

They want to live, and improve, Florence's home. Peter is selling his home. Both know that "if anything should happen, if one of us dies", their own children should inherit their estates. Peter's daughter has mixed feelings towards Florence, and feels that the marriage is a "rebound relationship". Florence's son is studying family law and is always "advising" her about equalization payments and support, and the like. And Florence worries about Larry.

THEIR CONCERNS

"How can we share some assets, and preserve other assets for our own children?"

They ask about powers of attorney.

Florence wants to set-up a fund for Larry - it's too much for him to control his own money.

And, like everyone, they ask about taxes.

THE PLAN

They decide on the following objectives:

- Florence's home is worth about $200,000. It needs repair and improvement. Peter will contribute the $100,000 to do so. When the improvements are made to Florence's home, she will have a two-thirds interest, and Peter will have a one-third interest. They will share in the market value in proportion to their interests. The value of the home will vary with the market. If they later contribute to major repairs or improvements other than according to their interests, their interests are to be adjusted to take account of it. They want the survivor to be able to live in it, but they want their interests in it ultimately to go to their own children.
- Their bank accounts are to go to the survivor.

- Their combined RRSP's and pension benefits will be enough to look after the survivor. The survivor will pay the tax as the funds are withdrawn. When the survivor dies, any remaining RRSP value is to be divided equally between the two families.
- The rest of their assets, including their life insurance, will go to their own families.
- Because the court costs could be substantial, they would like to arrange that their executors do not need to probate their Wills.

They would like to arrange that their survivor would not be able to give the other's assets to someone other than the other's children. (This is a common objective; even in the happiest of families, it is usually best to assume that children of different parents should not have to look to the goodwill of a surviving step-parent to receive what their own parent wanted to leave them.)

COMMENTS

Tax

When he sells it, any gain-over-cost in the value of Peter's present home will not be taxed because it is his principal residence. A gain in their interests in Florence's home will not be taxed because it will be their principal residence. RRSP's and survivor pension benefits that go to a surviving spouse are not taxed when the first one dies; the tax will be paid as the spouse withdraws the funds; when the survivor dies, the remaining values will be taxed in the survivor's at-death tax return. Tax on RRSP's is at full income rates, not at capital gains rates. Most life insurance proceeds are not taxed.

When each of them dies, any untaxed gains on the other assets will be taxed. They could have put the other assets in a "spouse trust" for the survivor - all the income and discretionary capital to the survivor during his or her life - but they decided to pay the tax so that their children wouldn't have to wait until the survivor dies.

Probate Court Fees

The court fees will be paid if their Wills need to be probated. The issue is to look at the assets to see if there are ways to place the assets in the executors' or the beneficiaries' hands without probate of the Will.

THE DOCUMENTS

Florence's Home

- Register title in both names jointly.
- Complete a marriage contract that sets out their contributions and percentage interests, that provides for varying their interests if they later contribute other than according to their interests, that the survivor by surviving does not own the other's interest in the home, that as long as the survivor wants to do so the survivor is entitled to live in the home with the survivor to pay the insurance, taxes and other upkeep costs; that they and the survivor will share the sale proceeds in proportion to their interests (the survivor will pay the other's share of the proceeds to the other's children or estate). A contract cannot be changed by the survivor; it is binding on the survivor and for the benefit of the other's children. For the domestic contract, they each need independent legal advice. This includes full financial disclosure by each to the other.

Bank Accounts

They can change the accounts to joint accounts.

RRSP Beneficiary Designations

In the plans, they can designate the other to receive the RRSP death benefits. Because the survivor's plans may leave a death benefit and they want it to be divided between the two families, in their designations in the plans, they can designate the survivor's estate as the alternate beneficiary, and the survivor's Will can divide the after-tax benefit equally. But that may require probate of the survivor's Will. Instead, in their designations in their plans, Peter and Florence can name their children and step-children, or a trustee for them, as the alternate beneficiaries of the proceeds, net of tax, to be divided equally by family (they can include the same provisions for gifts-over if a child dies prematurely).

Life Insurance

Each can name their estates as the beneficiary of their policies. But if this results in the insurer requiring probate of the Will, instead of naming the estate, each could name a person to hold the proceeds in trust as directed by the executors without requiring probate of the Will.

Probate

If Florence's home is registered jointly (subject to the off-title contract), if they make direct designations of beneficiaries of their life insurance (instead of their estates), and if they designate the beneficiaries (instead of their estates) in their RRSP's, there remains their portfolios of securities (including what Florence may inherit).

To deal with the portfolio securities, one or several names can be added to the account with the investment dealer. So that there is no change in beneficial ownership, the added persons will sign "non-beneficial acknowledgements" - acknowledgements that there is no change in beneficial ownership, that they will act as instructed by the owner, that they will act as instructed by the owners executors without needing probate of the Will, and they complete powers of attorney to the owner. Any change in beneficial ownership would result in a taxable transfer.

Their Wills and Powers of Attorney for Property

In their Wills, if the above steps are taken, they can leave the rest of their assets to their own children.

In her Will, Florence can set aside Larry's share in a discretionary trust, to be managed for him during his lifetime.

Peter and Florence can complete powers of attorney for property and for personal care.

14

The Family Business

In estate planning, the family business is one of the most difficult asset to deal with. Typically, one or a few persons start it, and own it. When they start the business, they are almost totally consumed with cash-flow; they have little time for anything else. Usually, they have no time for, or interest in, and don't want to pay for, long-term "estate planning" - looking to the future to the management and transfer of their assets when the business changes, or if they become disabled or die. While long-term decisions are delayed because of the short-term needs, the two are inextricably mixed.

There are two working regimes - the regime of those who work for others, for the organization; and the regime of those who work for themselves. Business regulatory systems are written primarily by and for those in the organization. Despite the fundamental differences, much of the regulation applies to small businesses. The "big" dominates the "small". The managing classes, and those who work for them, fundamentally do not comprehend those who create the "small".

Despite their number and importance, our middle-class self-employed struggle against the economic strength of the large organizations. Most new businesses fail - from lack of capital, from mismanagement. If they succeed, few of them successfully pass to the next generation.

This is fundamental to an understanding of long-term estate planning for the owners of small businesses. And because all their available capital has to be used for the business, the owners don't have much time or money for long-term personal planning. Unlike organizations and their managers, there is no separation between the owners and their small businesses. And somehow, the owners' advisors have to keep the long-term in mind; and to build in some long-term features while meeting the owners' immediate needs, and to do this with as little cost as possible.

This means several things: The accountants and lawyers have to be sensitive to the owners' obsession with the business, and have to economize their time, costs, and the language in their documents. Those who start and develop businesses have no trouble understanding issues and making decisions; and they do not want to deal with anything other than what they need to deal with. They are offended by bombast, puffery, legalese, complexity, and the unnecessary. They do not like to be patronized - particularly by professionals.

Professionals - accountants, lawyers, bankers, insurance agents, financial planners - involved in estate planning should work together, not independently. Every business, from beginning to end, needs an accountant. The lawyer should always work with the accountant and other professionals; not to do so may cause mistakes and confusion.

This book is written by lawyers. Our experience is that entrepreneurs detest documents that are taken from long precedents, badly written, contradictory, and contain far more than is needed. What is needed is the ability to listen, to write, to be patient, to decide what is important, and to prepare brief documents that can be read and understood. What is also needed is a quality, low-cost service.

The following example illustrates some long-term issues that occur at stages in the building of a business. Many more than those listed will occur. Those listed will occur at any stage, and not necessarily in the order outlined.

START-UP

Bob is 35, married, with two young children. He has worked in the telephone business for 10 years and is now starting his own telephone accessories business. With his accountant, he has prepared his business plan. It includes conservative and realistic expense and revenue projections, the value of his time, the capital needed and an estimated return on capital. He is obtaining capital from his savings and his wife's family. He has an accountant, a lawyer, and a banker.

Estate Planning Considerations

- Will he incorporate, or use a proprietorship? Considerations include: limited liability; tax consequences including the use of start-up losses, and the capital gains exemption of up to $500,000 for shares in a private active business corporation.

- If the business has substantial growth potential, does he want to share growth-ownership with his family by sharing with them the start-up shares in the corporation? If so, and if his children are to be shareholders, will he want a trust to hold their shares, and if so, what are the terms of the trust?
- What about life insurance? Does he want insurance to cover business liabilities, and if so will the premiums be tax-deductible? Will it be corporate-owned, or self-owned? Does he want life insurance outside the business that is not subject to claims by creditors? What about disability insurance?
- Does he want to protect his non-business assets from business liabilities? If so, how? By transferring them to his wife?
- What are the terms of the capital that he is obtaining? Will it be debt or equity?

If debt, what are the terms of repayment, security, and negative covenants?

If equity, and if it is going to be a partnership, will it be a limited partnership so that the investors will have limited liability? What are the priorities of the investor's partnership interests? Can Bob buy their interests; or is he obliged to do so, and if so, on what terms? How much control does Bob have? What are the management, and buy-sell provisions among the partners? What are the tax consequences?

If equity, and if he incorporates, how many shares will the investors receive? Will there be different classes of shares to contain the different equities? Will Bob have an option, or an obligation, to buy the investors' shares? Will the shareholders have pro-rata first rights to participate in additional financing? What control, voting, management, decision-making terms, and buy-sell provisions do they have? What are the tax consequences?

If he becomes incapable, who does he want to manage his business for him?

Documents

- Bob's Will: See the sample Will for a young couple, Chapter 17.
- Power of attorney for property: perhaps two - one for his business, the other for other assets, with neither cancelling the other.

- If debt financing: loan agreement, security interest document, registrations.
- For asset protection: transfer of assets to Bob's wife.
- If incorporation: private company provisions to comply with the "private issuer" securities-law prospectus/registration exemption (see below); shareholders' agreement.
- If a partnership: partnership agreement, registration.
- If life insurance: designations in the policies.

15 YEARS LATER

Unlike many start-ups, Bob has succeeded. He incorporated, and now he wants to expand the business. He needs more capital to finance the expansion. Again, he has a carefully prepared business plan. He also reviews his estate plan.

Estate Planning Considerations

- What are his sources of additional capital - the bank, other investors?
- Will the additional capital be debt or equity?

If debt, what are the terms, security and negative covenants?

If equity (shares in the corporation) from private investors or a venture capital firm, what are the terms of payment, control, priorities among shareholders, management, buy-sell obligations and options; pricing, life insurance for funding, representation on the board?

If equity, is the issue of shares exempt from the prospectus/registration requirements under the securities laws, such as under the "private issuer" exemption or the "seed capital" exemption?

In general, the private issuer exemption permits the trading in shares of a corporation without a prospectus if the transfer of shares is restricted and the number of shareholders does not exceed 50, and there is no offer of shares to the public.

In general, the "seed capital" exemption permits the offer of shares, once in the company's lifetime and if there is no advertising or promotional cost, to not more than 50 persons and subscriptions by not more than 25 subscribers, each of whom buys as principal, has access to prospectus-equivalent information, and due to his net-worth or independent advice from a registered dealer is able to evaluate the investment.

If the company stops being a private company, a report may have to be filed with the securities regulators; if the seed-capital exemption is used, a report must be filed with the regulators.

Note: At the time of writing, the Ontario Securities Commission has published a concept paper that discusses replacing four of the current "prospectus exemptions" (including the "private issuer exemption" and the "seed capital exemption") with two new exemptions: a "Closely-Held Issuer Exemption", and an "Accredited Investor Exemption". Persons involved with financing for companies will want to know the status of proposals by regulators to change present exemptions.

- Tax consequences: Does the corporation's financial position comply with the asset restriction for the capital gains exemption on shares of a small business corporation? If not, what redundant assets will be removed from the corporation, and how will this be done?
- Tax consequences: What is the tax on Bob's untaxed gain in his interest in the business? Where will the money come from to pay the tax? If there is real potential for further growth, does he want to fix the tax payable by transferring the future growth to his family? Even if there is no growth potential, does Bob want to restructure the corporation to share ownership with his wife and children?
- Does his life insurance need to be reviewed? If there is company-owned insurance on Bob's life, are the proceeds to be used to repay loans? Are any of the proceeds to be used to redeem Bob's shares?
- Do the earlier business agreements among the shareholders need to be reviewed?
- Does he need to review what will happen if he becomes incapable?
- What about Bob's retirement planning; does he have RRSP's, a pension plan? Does he consistently remove redundant assets from the business so that they can be invested separately?
- Is he still personally liable on any business debts, such as bank loans, and if so, can he be released from them?

Documents

- Bob's Will: Does he need special provisions to deal with the business? Does he want separate trustees to manage and dispose of the business? What special powers in the Will do the executor/trustees need? What instructions does he want to give to them, and how should he do so? Is there anyone who will have first rights, or an obligation, to buy the business, such as in a buy-sell agreement? If a child is to have the first chance to buy the business, what does Bob want to do, after providing for his wife, about equalizing his estate among his children, and what corporate restructuring is or will be needed, before or after he dies, to accomplish this? How much of this goes into his Will, and how much into other documents?
- Financing: share or debt documents, shareholder agreement, security instruments.
- Corporate restructuring: If the financing, or family participation involves reorganizing the issued and authorized shares, changes to the constating documents, and tax compliance.
- Life insurance designations.
- Powers of attorney for property and for personal care.
- Asset transfers to protect against business liabilities.

15 MORE YEARS LATER

Bob obtained his financing to expand. The business continues to prosper. It generates its own capital for expansion. It maintains a good rate of earnings and a sound balance sheet. Its asset coverage for its liabilities is sound. It has key-man life insurance on Bob to fund a repurchase or redemption of his shares. It distributes its redundant assets to its shareholders. It has good employees. Bob is now 65 and looking for a way out of the business — in part or in whole.

Estate Planning Considerations

- Is there a ready market for the business? Who are the potential buyers? Does he want to set up a sale to employees, or to a child?
- If it is a sale to employees, what are his post-closing obligations to the buyers, and what are the earn-out terms of the sale? What security is there for the deferred part of the purchase price? To reduce the assets being sold and therefore the price and risk, how

many corporate assets can be distributed to the shareholders before the sale?

- If there is a sale, will Bob sell his shares, or will the corporation sell its assets? What are the tax consequences of each method, and how do they affect the price?
- If a sale to employees or a child, what restructuring of the share capital is needed to accommodate the sale? What is the security for the deferred payments on the price?
- If it is a sale to a child, how will Bob secure a fair distribution out of the business to his wife if she survives him?
- If there is no ready buyer for the business, and if Bob wants some way for him, his family, and any other shareholders to be able to sell their shares, does he want to "take his company public"? What are the advantages and disadvantages?
  - Advantages: The ability to sell their shares in a public market, at a price determined by the market.
  - Disadvantages: The risk of not marketing the initial issue after the substantial cost of disclosure and distribution compliance; the high cost of continuing public disclosure and securities regulatory compliance.
- Does Bob want, before he dies, to facilitate the at-death transfer of his business and other assets to his family, and does he want an uninterrupted management of his assets through his old age and his death?

  If so, will an inter-vivos trust accomplish this? What are advantages and disadvantages?
  - Advantages: The cost of setting up and administering the trust will probably be considerably less than the cost of setting up and administering the estate. He will be one of the trustees; the succession of trustees will be set out in the trust document; he will co-manage with the other trustees, and they will continue in office when he becomes incapable or dies. The trust will say how the assets are to be distributed after he dies (in the same way as in his Will). Because the trust governs the management and distribution of the assets that are in the trust, his Will does not govern such assets, and probate of his Will is not needed to deal with such assets.
  - Disadvantages: The cost to set up and administer the trust is incurred while he is alive; the cost to administer his Will would be incurred when he dies. If he wants to transfer assets that

have untaxed gains to the trust, the structure to do so without attracting premature payment of the tax could be complicated.

To facilitate the at-death transfer, does Bob want his wife to become a joint owner of any of his assets? If not his wife, is there a child or other person who would become a joint owner; and is the name added to facilitate the at-death transfer and not to transfer any beneficial interest?

- If Bob dies before the business is sold, and if it is not a public company, does he want a child or an employee to have the first opportunity to acquire the business? If a child, how will he secure an appropriate distribution out of the business to his wife if she survives him; how does he want to ultimately treat his children equally?
- Review current tax considerations, powers of attorney for property and for care, insurance and RRSP designations.

Documents

- Corporate restructuring to accommodate a buyer.
- Will: Instructions regarding the first opportunity to an employee or a child to acquire the business that include pricing, payment and control of the business; if there is a spouse-trust, defining what the "income" of the business will be and the methods of securing it; restructuring the share capital to provide for participating equity by other children to ultimately share equally.
- Powers of attorney for property, and for care.
- Life insurance and RRSP and pension designations.
- Inter-vivos trust: the trust agreement, the asset transfers, tax compliance.

PART IV
Precedents

15

Drafting Documents

The samples in the following chapters are just that - samples; illustrations. They should be adapted to meet the circumstances.

The Will and the trust are "charter" documents; they are akin to articles of incorporation and by-laws of a corporation. They tell the trustees and the executors what they are to do and when and how they are to do it. They may not be the only document to do so; they may stand alone, or together, or along with marriage contracts (such as in second marriages), contracts (such as buy-sell arrangements for family-owned businesses), and RRSP and life insurance designations.

STRUCTURE

First, establish the structure for the document. Decide what it is to do.

A Will usually does these things:

- It names the executor/trustees.
- It tells them to pay debts.
- It tells them to distribute what is left among the beneficiaries.
- It may have something to say about who qualifies as children (adoption in and out, legitimacy), and the protection of benefits to beneficiaries against marriage breakdown.
- It gives them the tools to do the job.

Estates have one or more phases. The first phase is the "executors' year" - the time needed to gather in the assets, to determine and provide for the liabilities and costs, and to distribute the balance. Later stages are for ongoing trusts, such as for the surviving spouse, and for children. The estate for which you are doing the Will may have only one phase, or it may have more. The executor in the first phase is a fiduciary. So are the trustees of ongoing trusts. But, for both reporting to beneficiaries and for tax-reporting, they account separately for each phase, and for each ongoing trust, both for reporting to beneficiaries and for tax-reporting. And the executors may not be the same as the trustees of the ongoing trusts, and the trustees of ongoing trusts may not be the same.

So, in your structure, separate these phases.

Also, keep in mind that testators should tell the trustees of the ongoing trust what they are to do. The testators allocate assets to the trust. They tell the trustees who the beneficiaries are. They tell the trustees when the trust ends, that is when to finally distribute what is left of the assets. They tell the trustees how to allocate income and capital in the meantime. They tell the trustees when and how to close "classes" of beneficiaries (for example - "equally per stirpes among my issue alive when my spouse dies").

The structure of the trust is like that of the Will. The trust names the trustees, the assets in the trust, the beneficiaries, and tells the trustees what to do, and when and how to do it. It deals with the powers and succession of the trustees.

PLAIN LANGUAGE

The Will that you draw should tell the executor/trustees what they are to do, and who will benefit and when. Do it in plain language. This is not easy. To write in plain language is to force yourself to think about what you are to say, and how to say it. If you develop your own plain-language precedents, if you know what every word in them means and when to use and adapt the bits and pieces, your confidence in what you do will increase, you will save time, you will do a better job, and you will rely less on precedents that others pass on to you.

To write a document in plain language is to set out only the essential information in a way that gives the reader a good chance, at first reading, of understanding it, and with the meaning that you intend. This is not a new idea.

Chaucer had one of his characters say: "Speketh so pleyne at this time, I yow preye, that we may understande what ye seye". In 1550, Edward VI became so exasperated with the law that he said, "I would wish that the superfluous and tedious statutes were made more plain and short, to the intent that men might better understand them."

In the nineteenth century, Jeremy Bentham described legal English as "excrementitious garbage". Has it changed? As lawyers, do we wrap legal mysteries in unusual language. Legalese brings lawyers into disrepute. Many lawyers despise it, many campaign for plain language. If we want to win the readers' confidence, we should give them understandable documents to sign.

Research shows that documents crafted in plain language improve the readers' understanding.

Do not confuse plain language with a lack of style. Only by using plain language can you develop your own style, for a trust or a Will or any other document. You have to learn and practice the craft of plain writing; but, like other crafts, excellence is hard to achieve, few of us achieve it.

Some tips: These apply to all legal writing, not just to trusts and Wills. Start by writing down the points - first the main ones, then the sub-points. This will look like a tree. This is the structure. As you do this, you will think of things that you have forgotten, or are not needed, and you can change your structure.

- Expand each point and sub-point.
- Don't use long sentences. Break up long sentences into short ones.
- Use words that the readers will understand.
- Don't use unnecessary words.
- Prefer the active voice, unless there's a good reason to use the passive.
- Use the correct verb.
- Make the proper connections between nouns and pronouns.
- Use vertical lists to break up complicated text.
- Reduce cross-references to a minimum.
- Avoid sexist language.
- Use accurate punctuation.
- Use a clear layout.

- Replace or eliminate legalisms.
- Practice, practice, practice.

16

Sample Will for an Older Couple with Children and Grandchildren

John and Mary Jones have three adult children and some grandchildren. They want to leave everything to their survivor, and then to their children. This is John's Will; Mary's would be its mirror.

This sample has a structure. In sequence, John names the executors; then tells them what to do: pay debts, pay a legacy, give the rest to Mary if she survives; if she doesn't, divide the personal effects, give a legacy, and divide what is left equally among the children, with a gift-over to children of a deceased child. And it attaches a list of administrative powers for the executors. Comments are in *italics*.

WILL

I, John Jones, of Surreyville, Ontario, make this as my Will.

Under the Succession Law Reform Act (Ontario), a "Will" includes a "testament", a codicil, an appointment by Will in the nature of a Will in exercise of a power, and any other testamentary disposition.

1. I appoint my wife Mary Jones (Mary) as my executor/trustee. If she does not survive me, or is unable or declines to act, or having accepted the appointment ceases to act as my executor/trustee, I appoint my children Barbara Jones (Barbara), Maxwell Jones (Max) and Edith Brown (Edith) my executor/trustees. Please

In Ontario, the executor is also called the estate trustee with a will. "Probate" is now called a "Certificate of Appointment of Estate Trustee". (An administrator is now called an estate trustee without a will.) The executor completes the first, and perhaps the only, phase in the administration of an estate; a trustee deal with my estate as follows.

manages an ongoing testamentary trust. This clause does not refer to 30 days or some other time for the executor to survive the deceased. It does provide for succession of executorship in several situations. See Chapter 8, "Estate Administration". Also see Chapter 4, "The Will", under "Who are the executors?". John and Mary may want someone to act with Mary if she survives John.

(Later, "you" means the executor/trustees, and includes trustees appointed under paragraph 12 of the Schedule; a grandchild or great-grandchild of mine means someone (i) who is a blood descendant of mine whether or not he or she is adopted by someone else, and (ii) who is adopted by a child or other blood descendant of mine.)

To make it easier to read, you may want to use definitions. This sample talks to "you", the executors, and the trustees of an ongoing testamentary trust. This is common in plain-language contracts and documents.

2. Pay my debts and taxes, my funeral expenses, the cost to administer my estate, and any estate, inheritance and succession taxes and duties that are payable because of my death.

Note that income taxes are a debt; that is tax up to the date of death is a debt of the deceased. The tax for the "executor's year" may be a debt of the general estate, according to the tax-plan for the administration of the estate. See Chapter 11, "Taxes, Canadian and Foreign" about who is to pay the tax. To make it clear to the executor, you may want to also say that the general costs are to be charged to the general estate, and the costs of an ongoing testamentary trust are to be charged to that trust. At present, there are no inheritance and estate taxes in Canada (instead there are deemed at-death capital gains.) But there are estate taxes in the US, and in other countries.

3. Give $5,000 to the Surreyville Food Bank.

This legacy takes effect whether or not Mary survives John.

4. Give the remainder of my estate to Mary if she survives me by thirty days.

This clause leaves it to the surviving spouse outright; see below, for an alternate clause for a "spouse trust". Make it clear that "remainder" (some say "residue") applies throughout the Will. Here, it means what is left over after the debts and other items in clause 2 and 3 are provided for.

5. If Mary does not survive me by thirty days, distribute the remainder of my estate as follows:

We are dealing with the same "remainder" as in clause 4.

(a) Divide my personal and household effects, including jewellery, paintings, art objects, cars and boats, among my family as you decide. Please be guided by any memoranda I may leave about this.

This gives the executors the discretion to make this distribution. The testator should express the memo as a guide, not enforceable instructions; otherwise the memo becomes a "Will". Many testators want something different - direct bequests in the Will that can only be changed by a codicil, or a plan for equal-value distribution. So vary this clause to meet the circumstances.

(b) Give $1,000 to my sister, Jean Smithers if she survives Mary and me.

In this sample, this legacy takes effect only if John survives Mary.

(c) Divide the balance of the remainder of my estate equally among those of Barbara, Max and Edith who survive me, except that if any of them dies before me leaving a child or children who survive me (including one conceived and born later), divide what my deceased child would have received equally among his or her children who survive Mary and me.

Barbara, Max and Edith are named in Clause 1. Here we are talking not about the remainder, but about the balance of the remainder - the remainder less the personal and household effects and the legacy to Jean. A shorter way is to say to divide it "equally per stirpes among my issue". But non-lawyers don't know what this means. Also, this makes it clear that a conceived but unborn child is included in the class. The class of children of a deceased child closes on the death of the survivor of John and Mary. Instead of the gift-over to children of a deceased child, John might prefer to leave it to the child to decide what is to be done if the child dies prematurely; that is, John could give his children a power to appoint their share if the child dies prematurely.

(d) If a grandchild of mine is to receive part of my estate and is under age twenty-one, you are to set that part aside and hold it in a trust fund on these terms.

Unless there are trusts for them in the Will, shares to minors are paid into, and administered by, the court. This sample assumes that the testator's children are adults. This sample also uses age twenty-one.

Here, John could appoint someone other than the executors (the two remaining children if one of them dies prematurely) to manage this fund, and could tell the executors to transfer the fund to the other persons to hold in trust on the stated terms. Or John could direct the remaining executors to add the grandchild's other surviving parent as a trustee. Or, under clause 12 of the Schedule, the executors have discretion to do so.

You are to pay the balance of the fund to the grandchild when he or she reaches twenty-one. Before then, you may use the fund for the grandchild. For this purpose, you will decide how much of the fund to use, when to use it, and whether to pay amounts to the grandchild or to others on his or her behalf. You may use income of the fund or capital of the fund, as you choose. During a fiscal year of the fund you need not use anything, either income or capital (transfer income not used in a fiscal year of the fund to the capital). If this fund is still continuing twenty-one years after I die and if required by the law of accumulations to do so, starting twenty-one years after I die and after the grandchild reaches majority, pay all the income of the fund to the grandchild.

The "you" is the trustee - see above. This is a discretionary trust for the grandchild - the trustees decide how much capital and income to pay to the grandchild. This also deals with the Accumulations Act - include it only if needed.

If the grandchild dies before he or she reaches twenty-one, divide what is left of the fund when the grandchild dies equally among his or her children who are alive when the grandchild dies. If the grandchild does not leave a child or children, divide what is left of the fund equally among the grandchild's siblings who are alive when he or she dies. If the grandchild does not leave a sibling, divide what is left of the fund equally and by representation among my descendants who are alive when the grandchild dies.

This provides a "gift-over" if the grandchild dies before age 21. See Saunders v. Vautier under "The Trust". In the provinces where Saunders v. Vautier applies, if there is no gift-over, because the grandchild's interest would be fully vested, he or she can require payment at majority. Note also that the classes of siblings and descendants close when the grandchild dies.

6. If a person other than a grandchild of mine is to receive part of my estate and is under the age of majority, hold that part in a trust fund and pay the balance of the fund to the person when she or he reaches majority. Before then, from time to time as you decide, you may pay all, part or none of the income and capital of the fund to the person or for her or his benefit. Add income of the fund not so used during a year to the capital.

This is a standard trust for a minor, payable at majority. It is fully vested to the minor.

7. The income and the capital of a gift to a person under this Will shall not form part of the person's family property or matrimonial property or community property that may exist between the person and his or her spouse, and shall not, to the

See "Ontario Family Law Act". This clause excludes a gift from the beneficiary's family property to the extent permitted, and also deals with family-breakdown property under other regimes.

extent allowed by law, be subject to claims arising from the breakdown or termination of marriage or of a conjugal relationship.

8. You have the powers listed in the attached Schedule that I have initialled and is part of this Will.

In this sample, by putting them in a schedule, the "administrative" powers are separated from the dispositive part of the Will. This is a matter of style. Administrative and dispositive powers overlap; how assets are invested may affect how much income and capital beneficiaries receive.

9. I revoke all my previous Wills.

This isn't necessary - a later Will revokes an earlier one. But to put it in answers the inevitable question.

Date:

This is signed by John Jones and by us, all in the presence of each other.

The testator signs the Will in the presence of two witnesses present at the same time, and the witnesses subscribe in the presence of each other.

Signatures

SCHEDULE

You may do the following things when they do not conflict with what is in my Will and when you consider it to be in the best interest of the beneficiaries to do so. (These add to what you may do under the general law.)

This is a schedule of the administrative powers. Each page is initialled by the testator and the witnesses. These should be carefully reviewed to suit the Will. They are discretionary. Not all may be needed, but if something should be done, and it can't because the Will doesn't say so, it can be a problem.

1. You may deposit money and maintain accounts in a bank or a trust company.

2. You may sell assets that I own when I die. You may sell assets that you acquire after I die. You may sell assets for cash or credit on appropriate security. You may invest and reinvest in any investment that you consider prudent.

Become familiar with what the Trustee Act provides for "trustee investments'. Under this clause, the executor can sell real property, and doesn't have to rely on the Estates Administration Act.

3. As lessees, you may renew a lease held by the trust. As lessors, you may grant or renew a lease or sublease of property.

4. You may manage, maintain, repair, renovate, improve and develop property. You may insure property against loss, damage and any other risk.

5. You may vote and otherwise deal with shares and other securities as you see fit.

This is useful to make it clear that the executor can vote the deceased's shares.

6. You may borrow money and, as security, mortgage, pledge or otherwise charge assets.

7. You may contest or assert claims, settle debts and other matters relating to the assets and to the administration of the estate.

8. Instead of selling assets to realize money and then distributing only money to the beneficiaries, you may distribute estate assets to the beneficiaries as part or all of their shares in the estate; you may determine the fair market value of those assets and the value shall be binding on the beneficiaries.

This allows the executors to distribute "in specie", rather than selling everything and distributing cash.

9. If you are to give jewellery, paintings, art, or the like to someone under the age of majority, or if you are to pay money to someone under that age, you may do so by giving the article or by paying the money to his or her parent, or to the person who has custody of the child, or to the guardian of the child's property if there is one. That person's receipt will be a satisfactory discharge to you and that person will be responsible for giving the article or the money to the child when he or she reaches majority. Also, you may keep and store articles for the child until he or she reaches majority and you may charge the cost to do so to the general estate or to a trust for that child if there is one.

Minor's can't give valid receipts. This is permission to the executors to distribute what a minor is to receive to the minor's parent or guardian. This is useful for specific items and for small amounts of cash.

10. You may defer, pay by instalments, commute, or prepay death taxes and duties that are payable because of my death (the estate, gift, legacy, inheritance and

succession taxes and duties wherever charged).

11. You may make elections and take other steps under the *Income Tax Act* and other taxing statutes.

12. You may appoint one or more persons to act as a trustee or trustees of a trust fund to be established under my Will to add to the number of initial trustees, or to replace an executor who is unable or unwilling to act as a trustee of that fund. Thus, separate trust funds may have different trustees. This may be done by a deed signed by the executors and by the person or persons so appointed

This clause is to provide for succession of trustee management. The court has to replace an executor. But the court doesn't have to replace the trustee of an ongoing testamentary trust; the Will can provide for this.
This clause, for example, allows the executors to add a parent of a grandchild to that grandchild's trust (where the other parent died prematurely).

After a trust fund is established, the trustees (or the trustee if only one) of that trust fund may appoint one or more persons to act as a trustee or trustees of the trust fund to replace a trustee who retires, or to add a trustee or trustees. This may be done by a deed signed by the trustees and by the person or persons so appointed. Also, if there are two or more trustees, one may retire and be discharged from the trust; this shall be done by a deed signed by all the trustees, and a replacement trustee need not be appointed.

A new trustee appointed under the two preceding paragraphs shall have the same authority and powers as if originally appointed by me.

....

Clauses for a Spouse Trust

Instead of leaving everything outright to Mary if she survives him, John and Mary may want to leave a trust for Mary. They may want to do this for tax reasons, or Mary may not want (or may not be capable of) the sole responsibility of management. Or this may be a second marriage, and they may want to preserve what each has, while the survivor is alive, to give to their own children when the survivor dies. And if so, instead of naming Mary as the sole executor, John might name an additional executor.
The clause numbers correspond to the numbers in the above sample.

1. I appoint my wife Mary Jones (Mary) and my daughter Barbara Jones (Barbara) as my executor/trustees. If either of them does not survive me, or is unable or declines to act, or having accepted the appointment ceases to act as my executor/trustee, to replace her I appoint my children Maxwell Jones (Max) and Edith Brown (Edith) as additional executor/trustees. Please deal with my estate as follows.

John appoints both Mary and a child as co-executors.

4. If Mary survives me, set aside and hold the remainder of my estate in a trust fund on these terms:Pay Mary or to others for her benefit the income of the fund that arises after I die and up to when she dies. Also, from time to time in your discretion, you may pay all or part of the

For tax purposes, a "non-tainted" spouse trust has to provide that during the spouse's lifetime the spouse receives all the income, and no one else will receive capital. This clause says that she receives all the income and the trustees have discretion to pay capital to her. To preserve

capital of this fund to Mary or for her benefit.

capital, John and Mary may not want the ability to encroach on capital for Mary.

5. When the survivor of Mary and me dies, divide the remainder as follows.

Here add the clauses for personal and household effects, legacies, division among children, grandchildren.

17

Sample Will for a Young Couple with Children

John and Mary Jones have three young children. They want to leave everything to their survivor, and then they want what they leave to be held, in a single fund, for their children until the youngest reaches twenty-one. The sample is by the husband. The wife's Will will be the same with the appropriate name changes.

The comments in the previous sample apply here. Other comments are added in *italics*.

WILL

I, John Jones, of Surreyville, Ontario, make this as my Will.

1. I appoint my wife, Mary Jones (Mary), as my executor/trustee. If she does not survive me, or is unable or declines to act, or having accepted the appointment ceases to act as my executor/trustee, I appoint Mary's sister, Martha Brown, as my executor/trustee. Please deal with my estate as follows.

(Later, "you" means the executor/trustee, and includes a trustee appointed under paragraph 12 of the Schedule.)

2. Pay my debts and taxes, my funeral expenses, the cost to administer my estate, and any estate, inheritance and succession taxes and duties that are payable because of my death.

3. Give the remainder of my estate to Mary if she survives me by thirty days.

4. If Mary does not survive me by thirty days, distribute the remainder of my estate as follows:

(a) Divide my personal and household effects, including jewellery, paintings, art objects, cars and boats, among my family as you decide. Please be guided by any memoranda I may leave about this.

(b) Set aside the remainder of my estate and hold it in a trust fund for my children on the following terms (the "Children's Trust"): When the last of my surviving children reaches twenty-one, divide the then balance of the fund equally among my children who are then alive. Before then, you shall use the fund for my children and in the proportions between them as you decide. You need not

This is an ongoing trust. It states what goes into the trust. It names the children as the class of beneficiaries; it opens the class on John's death, and closes it when the youngest child reaches twenty-one. It tells the trustee what to do with the income and capital in the meantime. It tells the trustee that she does not need to treat the children equally so that she can deal with a child's sickness, special treat them equally; this is so that you can meet their individual circumstances. You will decide how much of the fund to use, when to use it, and whether to pay amounts to a child or to others on his or her behalf. You may use income or capital of the fund as you choose. During a fiscal year of the fund, you need not use anything - income or capital (transfer income not used in a fiscal year of the fund to the capital).

education, or other special needs.

(c) If a child of mine dies before the last of my surviving children reaches twenty-one, leaving his or her child or children who are then alive (including one conceived and born later), set aside the share that my deceased child would have received and hold it in a separate trust fund for his or her children. The terms of this separate trust shall be the same as for the Children's Trust, with necessary changes.

This is a gift-over of the share of a child who dies prematurely to that child's children. It, also, is a separate ongoing trust. It names the children of the deceased child as the class of beneficiaries. It opens and closes the class when the last of John's children reaches twenty-one. By reference, it adopts the provisions of the children's trust.

5. The income and the capital of a gift to a person under this Will shall not form part of the person's family property or matrimonial property or

community property that may exist between the person and his or her spouse, and shall not, to the extent allowed by law, be subject to claims arising from the breakdown or termination of marriage or of a conjugal relationship.

6. You have the powers listed in the attached Schedule that I have initialled and is part of this Will.

7. If both Mary and I die when our children are young, to the extent that I can do so, I appoint Mary's sister, Martha Brown, to have custody of the children.

This is a "custody" clause.

8. I revoke all my previous Wills.

Date and signing as in the sample for the older couple.

18

A Sample Inter-Vivos Trust

John and Mary Jones have decided to put some of their assets in a trust, while they are alive, for themselves and their children. They do this because these assets can be managed during the transition through their retirement, probable incapacity, and death, with the same distribution as in their Wills.

This is a sample form of inter-vivos trust. Change it to suit any relevant tax concerns. Assets in the trust would not be part of their estates that are governed by their Wills. Thus their Wills will deal with what is not in the trust.

Like the sample Will, this form has a structure. It names the trustees, has some meanings for clarity, tells the trustees who the beneficiaries are, how long the trust is to last, and who will receive what is left when the trust ends. And it has administrative powers in a schedule.

The comments in the sample Will also apply to this sample.

THE JONES FAMILY TRUST

Date:

To: John Jones, Mary Jones and Barbara Jones, Trustees

John and Mary are appointing themselves and Barbara as the trustees. Later, they say that if John and Mary no longer are trustees, Barbara is to appoint the other two children as trustees.

From: John Jones (John) and Mary Jones (Mary)

John and Mary are the "settlors".

1. This is to be known as "Jones Family Trust". The trust fund (the "Fund") includes the assets in the schedule, and such other assets, money and property that you may accept and is added to the Fund from time to time.

Give it a name. Sometimes, settlors will start a trust with a small donation or a coin. See the "three certainties" in Chapter 1, "The Trust".

2. Meanings:

- "We" means John and Mary. "You" means the Trustees.
- The "Beneficiaries" are John and Mary, and our children Barbara Jones (Barbara), Maxwell Jones (Max) and Edith Brown (Edith) and, as mentioned later, their children and grandchildren.
- "Child" and "grandchild" mean someone (i) who is a blood descendant of mine whether or not he or she is adopted by someone else, and (ii) who is adopted by a child or other blood descendant of mine.
- The "Distribution Date" is the earlier of when the last of Barbara, Max and Edith dies or such earlier date as the Trustees may determine in writing.
- The "Trustees" are the trustees from time to time in office whether original, additional or substituted by the terms of this document.

3. We transfer to you the assets listed in the attached schedule, to be held in trust by you as follows.

4. Before the Distribution Date, from time to time and in your full discretion, you are entitled to pay all or part of the income and capital of the Fund to, or to others for the benefit of, one or more Beneficiaries. You decide how much of the

This will vary according to what is wanted. This clause says that the income and capital can be "sprinkled" among all the family. Or John and Mary may want all the income, as well as more of the discretionary capital, to be will available only to them and their

Fund to use, when to use it, and how much to use for each Beneficiary. You do not need to treat them equally.

survivor, and if so this clause would be changed.

You are entitled to accumulate income and add it to the capital of the Fund, except that if the Fund is still continuing twenty-one years after the date of this document and if required by the law of accumulations to do so, divide all the income among the Beneficiaries in the proportions among them as you decide.

5. On the Distribution Date, divide the balance of the Fund equally among those of Barbara, Max and Edith who are then alive, except that if any of them dies before then leaving a child or children who survive the Distribution Date (including one conceived and born later), divide what my deceased child would have received equally among his or her children who are then alive.

Note that the class closes on the Distribution Date.

If a grandchild of mine is to receive part of the Fund and is under age twenty-one, you are to set that part aside and hold it in a trust fund on these terms.

You are to pay the balance of the fund to the grandchild when he or she reaches twenty-one.

Before then, you may use the fund for the grandchild. For this purpose, you will decide how much of the fund to use, when to use it, and whether to pay amounts to the grandchild or to others on his or her behalf; you may use income of the fund or capital of the fund, as you choose. During a fiscal year of the fund, you need not use anything, either income or capital (transfer income not used in a fiscal year of the fund to the capital). If this fund is still continuing twenty-one years after the date of this document and if required by the law of accumulations to do so, starting twenty-one years after the date of this document and after the grandchild reaches majority, pay all the income of the fund to the grandchild.

If the grandchild dies before he or she reaches twenty-one, divide what is left of the fund when the grandchild dies equally among his or her children who are alive when the grandchild dies. If the grandchild does not leave a child or children, divide what is left of the fund equally among the grandchild's siblings who are alive when he or she dies. If the grandchild does not leave a sibling, divide what is left of the fund equally and by representation among my

The class closes when the grandchild dies.

descendants who are alive when the grandchild dies.

If a person other than a grandchild of mine is to receive part of the Fund and is under the age of majority, hold that part in a trust fund and pay the balance of the fund to the person when she or he reaches majority. Before then, from time to time as you decide, you may pay all, part or none of the income and capital of the fund to the person or for her or his benefit. Add income of the fund not so used during a year to the capital.

6. You are the first Trustees. A Trustee may retire as such from the Fund, or from a fund set aside for a grandchild, on thirty days prior written notice to the other Trustees of the particular fund, or on such earlier notice as they may accept. A Trustee is deemed to retire if he or she is found to be incapable of managing property, is declared bankrupt, or insolvent, or, if the Trustee is a corporation, it enters into liquidation. The Trustees or remaining Trustee or Trustees, in writing, may appoint an additional Trustee or Trustees of the Fund or fund for a grandchild, and may replace a Trustee who retires. If both John and Mary cease being

This provides for succession of management, and that when John and Mary are no longer in control, the three children will take on responsibility, with Barbara as the "bridge".

Trustees, Barbara shall appoint Max and Edith to be Trustees to replace John and Mary.

7. A person's interest in the income and the capital of this trust and benefits paid to a person under this trust shall not form part of the person's family property or matrimonial property or community property that may exist between the person and his or her spouse, and shall not, to the extent allowed by law, be subject to claims arising from the breakdown or termination of marriage or of a conjugal relationship.

8. As Trustees, you have the administrative powers in the attached schedule.

9. None of the Fund shall revert to us. We are not able to revoke this trust.

10. The laws of Ontario govern this trust.

Signed:

______________________	______________________
witness	John Jones
______________________	______________________
witness	Mary Jones

Acknowledgement and Receipt:

We acknowledge receipt of the assets in the schedule and confirm that we will hold the Fund and act as Trustees as set out above.

______________________	______________________
witness	John Jones
______________________	______________________
witness	Mary Jones
______________________	______________________
witness	Barbara Jones

SCHEDULE OF ADMINISTRATIVE POWERS

This list differs, in some respects, from the list in the Will. As in the Will sample, review this list to see what is wanted, and what is not.

This tells you, the Trustees, what you may do in administering the Fund and a fund for a grandchild. You may do the following things when they do not conflict with what is in the attached trust agreement and when you consider it to be in the best interest of the beneficiaries to do so. (These add to what you may do under the general law.)

1. You may invest and reinvest in any investment that you consider prudent.

2. You may sell assets of the Fund for cash, or for credit with appropriate security, or for a combination of cash and credit. You may dispose of trust assets by exchange for other property. Where a trust asset is an undivided portion, you may agree to the

partition of the asset in which the portion is held.

3. As an investment of the trust, you may purchase insurance on the life of a beneficiary, or on the life of any person in whom a beneficiary has an insurable interest.

4. You may vote and otherwise deal with corporate shares and other corporate and government securities.

5. You may borrow money and, as security, you may mortgage, pledge or otherwise charge any of the trust assets.

6. You may contest or assert claims, settle debts and other matters relating to the trust assets.

7. Instead of selling trust assets to realize money and then distributing only money to the beneficiaries, you may distribute trust assets to the beneficiaries as part or all of their shares in the trust; you may determine the fair market value of that asset and the value shall be binding on the beneficiaries.

8. You may make elections and take other steps under the *Income Tax Act* (Canada) and other taxing statutes.

9. You may transfer assets of the Fund to a corporation that you control (you may form a corporation for this purpose) in return for securities of the corporation, and you may retain the securities as investments of the Fund.

Sometimes, over the life of a trust that could last a long time, assets may be reorganized by forming holding companies. This clause permits the trustees to do so.

10. You may deposit trust money in a bank or a trust company. You may authorize one or more of you, as trustees, to make arrangements and agreements with banks and trust companies as to advances, overdrafts and loans, and to manage, transact, and settle all manner of banking business, including the drawing of cheques, promissory notes and other negotiable instruments, and to adjust and settle accounts with any bank or trust company.

11. You may hold assets of the Fund in one or more of your names (if there is more than one trustee), or in the name of your nominee. You may open accounts with investment dealers and authorize one or more of you to deal with the investment dealers for the purpose of trading in and handling securities and moneys that are part of the Fund.

Here, we have the issue of trustees "delegating" their responsibilities. Usually, trustees can delegate administrative matters, but should continue to be responsible for policy.

12. You may obtain the advice and assistance, including investment counsel, that you need to carry out your duties; and, from

time to time, you may retain a trust company to act as your agent in the management of the Fund.

13. You do not have to give a bond or other security. If you act in good faith, you are not liable for any error in judgment. You are liable for deliberate misconduct. You are to be indemnified out of the Fund against all claims and losses arising from your office as trustee, other than those resulting from your deliberate misconduct.

These last two clauses are superfluous, but sometimes it's good to include this for non-lawyers to see.

SCHEDULE OF ASSETS

Here: list the assets transferred to the trustees.

19

The Non-Beneficial Transfer

This document can be used when, for convenience, someone is added as a joint owner to the title to make easier the transfer of assets on death. It can be used as an off-title acknowledgement for real estate, or a bank account, or anything else. It is to confirm that there is no transfer of beneficial interest. The person who is added to the title is simply the agent of the owner; the agent is to do what he or she is told by the owner or the owner's personal representatives.

The same thing can be done with any kind of non-beneficial transfer.

This sample is a non-beneficial transfer of a portfolio of securities by Pamela Brown of her account with her investment dealer to her children, Samuel and Martha.

ACKNOWLEDGEMENT AND POWER OF ATTORNEY

We, Samuel Brown and Martha Brown, the children of Pamela Brown, acknowledge that we are added to the names on our mother's account of her securities and funds with Profound Securities Inc. (the "Securities"). We are doing this as a convenience for our mother. She owns the Securities. We are not acquiring any beneficial interest in the Securities.

For this purpose, each of us confirms the following:

1. We have no beneficial interest in the Securities. We are recorded on the account for the benefit of our mother.
2. While our mother is alive, we will do all things regarding the Securities as she directs us.

3. When our mother dies, we will transfer the Securities as our mother's personal representatives direct us. For this purpose, to confirm our mother's appointment of her personal representatives, we will accept a notarially certified copy of our mother's last will, and will not require the personal representatives to obtain a court certificate of their appointment as the estate trustees.

And for this purpose, we complete the following power of attorney to our mother.

CONTINUING POWER OF ATTORNEY FOR THE SECURITIES

Each of us, Samuel Brown and Martha Brown, irrevocably appoints our mother, Pamela Brown, to be her and his attorney for property regarding the securities and funds that our mother has with Profound Securities Inc. (the "Securities").

Each of us authorizes our mother, on our behalf and in our name, to sign, execute and deliver any and all transfers and other documents having to do with the Securities.

Each of us confirms that this power of attorney may be exercised during his or her incapacity.

We are not able to revoke this power of attorney by executing another power of attorney. Each of us confirms that if he or she executes a later power of attorney for property, it will not revoke this power of attorney.

Date:

________________________ ________________________

Samuel Brown Martha Brown

The following witness the signatures of the above two persons.

________________________ ________________________

Name and address Name and address

20

Continuing Power of Attorney for Financial Matters

This sample of a continuing power of attorney to deal with financial matters is modelled under the Ontario *Substitute Decisions Act, 1992*.

This should be changed to meet the circumstances. For example, the attorneys may be authorized to act separately, as well as together, and if so, it would say "jointly and severally". There may be restrictions on what the attorneys can do - perhaps as to the kind of investments that the attorney can make. Clause 3 contemplates other powers of attorney that exist and are to be left in place. The *Substitute Decisions Act, 1992* provides for compensation, but John Jones may want to say something special about this. Or John may want this to take effect only if he becomes incapable, and if so, there should be some way, set out in the document, to decide how he becomes incapable so that third parties can know that the power of attorney takes effect.

CONTINUING POWER OF ATTORNEY FOR PROPERTY

This continuing power of attorney for the management of property is given by JOHN JONES of Surreyville, Ontario.

1. I appoint my wife, Mary Jones, and my daughter, Barbara Jones, jointly, to be my attorneys

This says that they are to act jointly. If they are to be able to act separately, as well as jointly, for property in accordance with the *Substitute Decisions Act, 1992* to make decisions on my behalf concerning the management of my property and to do on my behalf anything that I could lawfully do except make a Will (my "attorneys").

substitute "jointly and severally" for "jointly".

2. This power of attorney may be exercised if I become incapable of managing property.

How are third parties to know that John becomes incapable? Here, someone, or several persons, could be appointed to make that decision which would be valid for third parties.

3. Except [*put here the power of attorney not to be revoked*] for which I do not revoke, I revoke all former continuing powers of attorney for the management of property.

There may be an earlier power of attorney for a specific purpose that John does not want to revoke.

4. I authorize my attorney to take compensation as set out in the *Substitute Decisions Act, 1992.*

This clause may be unnecessary. And see Chapter 2, "The Continuing Power of Attorney for Property".

Date:

____

John Jones

____________________ ____________________

Name and address | Name and address

21

Power of Attorney for Personal Care, the "Living Will"

This sample, modelled under the Ontario *Substitute Decisions Act, 1992*, appoints an attorney for personal care, and includes a brief statement of how certain decisions are to be made (a "living will"). It can take effect only if the donor becomes incapable of making these decisions.

This should be changed to meet the circumstances. Clause 1 appoints John's wife, Mary, as the attorney. The alternative clause 1 says that if Mary can't act, the children are appointed and they act jointly and severally.

A power of attorney for care and the living will, for many people, raise sensitive and difficult issues - the meaning and implications of different kinds of medical treatment; how and when to move the "aged parent" or spouse out of the house and into a retirement or nursing home. The actual power of attorney and wish statement should be prepared only after John and Mary have been able to make carefully considered decisions.

POWER OF ATTORNEY FOR PERSONAL CARE

This power of attorney for personal care is given by JOHN JONES of Surreyville, Ontario.

1. I appoint my wife, Mary Jones, and our children, Barbara Jones, Maxwell Jones

This appoints the four, jointly and severally.

and Edith Brown, jointly and severally, to be my attorneys for personal care in accordance with the *Substitute Decisions Act, 1992* to make decisions on my behalf with respect to my personal care if I am incapable of personal care decisions (my "attorneys").

1. I appoint my wife, Mary Jones, or if she dies before me or resigns or is otherwise unable or unable to act, I appoint our children, Barbara Jones, Maxwell Jones and Edith Brown, jointly and severally, to be my attorneys for personal care in accordance with the *Substitute Decisions Act, 1992* to make decisions on my behalf with respect to my personal care if I am incapable of personal care decisions (my "attorneys").

This is an alternative clause. It appoints Mary, with the children as alternates if Mary can't act.

2. I authorize my attorneys to take compensation as set out in the *Substitute Decisions Act, 1992*.

This may be unnecessary.

3. I do not want you to use life support systems or to take extreme measures to prolong my life if there is no reasonable possible hope of my recovery. In those circumstances, please allow me to die a natural death with a minimum of pain and anxiety.

This is the "living Will" part of the documents.

Date:

____

John Jones

________________________ ________________________

Name and address Name and address

INDEX

[The references in this table are to page numbers.]

W